THE FEAR
OF
THE LORD

The Beginning of Discipleship

BY

DAVID HOFFMAN

FOREWORD

After thirty-five years of full-time ministry, you develop a certain discernment as to the reality and relevance of different men and their ministry. In *The Fear of the Lord* David Hoffman has clearly been able to bridge the gap between an enigmatic and widely misunderstood truth and what the basic understanding and application of solid biblical truth can accomplish in daily life when properly applied.

This book is a must for those who desire to step into another dimension of holiness and obedience in every aspect of their life.

Pastor Bill Wilson
Metro Ministries, Brooklyn, New York

INTRODUCTION

SPECIAL STUDY GUIDE ENCLOSED

The Fear of the Lord has been written to be used as an individual study, or for study in a Home Fellowship, Group Bible Study or Sunday School Class. A special Study Guide section, complete with questions, is located in the back of this book, starting on page 251.

The Study Guide is designed to encourage individual growth or group participation. If you follow the Study Guide format, The Fear of the Lord Bible Study can be completed in seven weeks.

If you are a Group Bible Study leader or Sunday School teacher, you will find this book extremely "user friendly". The questions contained in this Study Guide target personal growth and understanding, and are easily answered without overwhelming the readers.

TABLE OF CONTENTS

THE FEAR OF THE LORD

The Beginning of Discipleship

BY

DAVID HOFFMAN

CHAPTER ONE

The Fear of the Lord Produces Knowledge and Wisdom

The fear of the LORD is the beginning of wisdom, And the knowledge of the Holy One is understanding.
[Proverbs 9:10]

Is your life built on preferences or convictions? A preference is something you greatly value or hold to as a high priority... something you *prefer*. A conviction is something to which you are deeply committed. A person with a <u>*preference*</u> for honesty might be willing to report wrong information on tax returns if it means saving several hundred dollars. They *prefer* to be honest, but are willing to compromise when it seems to be in their best interest to do so. A person with a <u>*conviction*</u> about honesty will report tax returns accurately—even if it means paying several thousand dollars more! That person is *committed* to honesty in spite of what it may cost them.

In the life of a Christian, the difference between a preference and a conviction is the fear of the Lord!

I believe the fear of the Lord is the most important Christian discipline you can develop. When you fear God, you provide Him with the platform from which He can protect and bless you. Sadly, the Church of Christ is overflowing with people who have a great number of preferences but very few convictions, revealing a great lack of the fear of God in their lives.

I have been a pastor for more than 20 years and have watched countless times as Christians willfully compromise and rationalize the Word of God so they can pursue their own desires instead of obeying God's decrees. For many years I thought I knew better than God what was good for me. As a result, I have suffered immensely at my own hand and have learned through hardship and disappointment that God's rules are designed to benefit His people...not to deprive them! All too often Christians distort, compromise and rationalize the word of God so they can justify pursuing their own desires. Too often their Christianity looks like this:

"This marriage is over! I have struggled for years to make it work, and instead I am miserable! Divorce is the only way I'll ever have real peace and happiness. God loves me and He wants me to be happy. I believe God will understand why I must get divorced even though there are no biblical grounds. In fact, I think He wants this for me, and even if I'm wrong I know God will forgive me."

"Pastor, I'm a businessman. I can't be completely honest. If I don't stretch the truth a little bit I'm not going to make any money! You just don't understand."

"I like to dress this way. Not to attract boys...I just like to be trendy and stay fashionable."

"I know I'm supposed to be the spiritual leader of my house, but it's such a hassle! Whenever I've tried to lead family devotions no one wants to follow me; it's just not worth it! Besides, I'm trusting God to lead them."

"Sure, I'd love to be involved in my children's education but I just don't have the time to do it. I'm far too busy just working to support them."

"Tithe? Have you see my bills? I can't afford to tithe! Besides, tithing is just an Old Testament requirement."

"If I take a stand on that issue, people will think I'm narrow-minded. They'll think I'm a Jesus freak. I could even get fired from work."

On and on it goes.

We compromise and rationalize the Word of God to obtain what we want. That is American Christianity. I must confess that I've compromised and rationalized the Word of God to justify all manner of things I wanted. In truth, I did not really believe the Bible, or I would have obeyed and not compromised. I *said* I believed the Word...I even *believed* I believed it. My choices proved otherwise.

When my idea of what I needed was different than what God said I needed, my actions proclaimed my unbelief. Had I *truly* believed God's Word, I would have obeyed Him.

I would have *feared the Lord*.

Learning to Fear the Lord

The Bible says that fearing the Lord is something you have to *learn* [Deut. 4:10; 14:23 and 17:19]. It does not come by osmosis. I put off writing this book for more than two years because I knew it would undoubtedly mean making changes in my life.

I liked my life. Church was going well, family life was good, I was building a new house! I had it made! Fearing God, a very serious undertaking, would mean a deeper commitment to Him. I know from experience that the more I commit myself to Jesus, the more I understand His Word, the less freedom I have to rationalize...and that usually means some things I enjoy are no longer acceptable.

The Bible is very clear: the more you know, the more you become accountable [Luke 12:47-48; Hebrews 10:26-31].

Consequence for Disobedience

As my commitment to Jesus and my knowledge of His Word have grown, so has my ability to see the consequences for disobedience. Being a pastor certainly has helped me learn to fear the Lord. I have the unique opportunity to see consequences surface in the lives of other people as if I am watching a movie. The plot unfolds right before my eyes. Time and time again I see people reaping the consequences of doing things their way instead of God's. If there is anyone who has good cause to fear the Lord (as I've seen people suffer consequences for disobedience) it is me! On the other hand, I have seen the blessings that come when someone fears the Lord and obeys Him.

It All Begins With FEAR

Consider what King Solomon is saying in the two scriptures below:

The fear of the Lord is the beginning of knowledge; fools despise wisdom and instruction. [Proverbs 1:7]

The fear of the Lord is the beginning of wisdom and the knowledge of the holy one is understanding.
[Proverbs 9:10]

If you belong to God, His plan for you is a life of blessing. Fearing Him is the *beginning* of that blessing. First, you need to know God's instructions for your life and His word...that is *knowledge*...but knowledge alone is useless. *Wisdom* is needed to give knowledge potential. Wisdom is the ability to apply what you know and understand, and the result is blessing. So then, an important question to ask is: "How do I acquire knowledge and wisdom?"

By fearing the Lord! Fearing the Lord is the *beginning!*

Knowledge is Never Enough

Please understand that wisdom and knowledge are not the same things. You may have plenty of knowledge, but if you do not have the wisdom to use your knowledge, it is useless.

I attended graduate school at San Diego State University where many of the professors possessed immense knowledge. My statistics teacher certainly had more than I could comprehend! She would begin writing a single equation on one side of the blackboard and continue all the way to the other side! Each day after class I went home, fell on my knees and cried, "Lord, You've got to help me! There is no possible way I can make it through statistics on my own!" It was only by God's grace that my final grade in that class was a B. I did not have my professor's vast knowledge of statistics, but I had enough wisdom to appeal to the One who could get me through the class.

I also attended a liberal seminary. Most of the professors were brilliant! They devoted their entire lives to study. They were proficient in Hebrew and Greek! But they were certainly not people you could go to for counsel or direction. Many of their lives were a mess. They had mind-boggling knowledge but no wisdom. Ironically, much of the knowledge these professors possessed was *biblical* knowledge, but without the wisdom to apply it to their lives. It was virtually useless to them!

Sadly, the American Church suffers in the same way. Christians are overflowing with knowledge but lack the wisdom to use it in everyday life.

1 Corinthians 8:1 says, *"Knowledge makes arrogant, but love edifies."* Knowledge alone may cause a person to puff up with pride, thinking, "I know all about this, I'm well educated and can handle it myself!" Placing confidence in knowledge can be dangerous.

On the other hand, knowledge in its proper place can be a source of godliness.

> *Paul, a bond-servant of God, and an apostle of Jesus Christ, for the faith of those chosen of God and the knowledge of the truth which is according to godliness.*
> *[Titus 1:1]*

Paul essentially is saying that knowledge can be a pathway to godliness. The key is having wisdom for a roadmap. An important question to ask yourself is, "What am I doing with the knowledge I have? Do I twist scripture to fit my preferences? Or do I know the fear of the Lord, draw my convictions from His Word and allow Him to direct me in wisdom?"

Christians who lack wisdom may gain all the knowledge in the world, but will still forfeit much of what Jesus came to provide for them:

> *The thief comes only to steal and kill and destroy:* ***I came that they may have life, and may have it abundantly.***
> *[John 10:10]*

If you are a Christian who lacks wisdom, you will fail to mature into the person God has purposed you to be. You will have salvation but forfeit much of the inheritance God has prepared for you here on earth!

You will have life eternally, but here on earth you will not have life abundantly.

Knowledge: A Tool for The Enemy

Knowledge is a blessing if you have the wisdom to use it properly, but it can also be a tool for the enemy. Look at John 10:10 again with a slightly different emphasis:

> ***The thief comes only to steal and kill and destroy:*** *I came that they may have life, and may have it abundantly.*
> *[John 10:10]*

Now consider Jesus' words in this example: two people attend medical school for many years and both become capable doctors. The first doctor has great knowledge but lacks wisdom. He employs his knowledge and uses his special skills every day as he performs abortions. The second doctor has great knowledge and skill, but he also has wisdom. He chooses to use his knowledge to save lives.

In the example of the first doctor, the "thief" succeeded in his plan to kill, steal and destroy because the doctor lacked wisdom. The "thief" stole the value of the doctor's special skills, killed an innocent child and destroyed at least three lives in the process: doctor, child and mother.

The second doctor's wisdom resulted in abundant life for both patient and doctor. "How could saving lives bring abundant life to the doctor?" you might ask. I believe it does! Even if the doctor is not a Christian, God blesses the physician's use of wisdom to do good works with his special skills. And one thing is certain: unlike the first doctor, he will not stand before God one day and explain why he willingly murdered helpless children.

Benefits of Fearing the Lord

The dictionary defines wisdom as *"true and right discernment, practical judgment, the ability to decide a course of action."* This is a real need in the Church today.

According to scripture, when you fear the Lord you acquire wisdom, and that leads to a life of blessing, peace, comfort, protection and victory. Let's examine Psalm 112 verse by verse to see some of the benefits of fearing the Lord:

> Verse 1: *"Praise the Lord! How blessed is the man who fears the Lord, who greatly delights in His commandments."*

Fearing God develops wisdom, and wisdom prompts you to obey God. Obedience bring blessing! Obeying God may begin as a desire to avoid consequences for disobedience, but as you experience blessing you grow to *delight* in His commandments! You gain greater insight into God's Word and that offers new opportunities to apply wisdom, resulting in more blessing. The cycle repeats as you continue to fear the Lord.

> Verse 2: *"His descendants will be mighty on earth; the generation of the upright will be blessed."*

When you fear the Lord, your children and their children will be blessed and so will others around you...your co-workers, people in your neighborhood and your community...will be blessed.

> Verse 3: *"Wealth and riches are in his house, and his righteousness endures forever."*

You will prosper! This does not mean that you are guaranteed to become rich...no scripture in the Bible promises that! Your life, however, will steadily improve as you obey God with your finances. Two years, five years, ten years down the road you are going to be better off than if you do not obey God in the way you handle money.

Verse 4:   *"Light arises in the darkness for the upright. He is gracious, compassionate and righteous."*

When you fear God you are like a flare in the darkness. The path is illuminated for you, and for you to lead the way for others. As you take on more of His traits, you become more gracious and compassionate.

Verse 5:   *"It is well with the man who is gracious and lends; He will maintain his cause in judgment."*

In other words, if you fear God your life will be marked by peace. You will not worry about finances, but find joy in the opportunities you have to give to others. Then, when you are in need, God will act on your behalf!

Verse 6:   *"For he will never be shaken; the righteous will be remembered forever."*

No matter what storm blows your way...when you fear God you will not be anxious! You know God is on the throne; He will give you direction and deliver you. Fear of the Lord causes you to trust Him despite circumstances. Trust is the anchor that keeps you from capsizing when the storms of life hit. Like so many god-fearing people before you, your life will be an inspiration to others long after you are gone.

Verse 7:   *"He will not fear evil tidings; His heart is steadfast, trusting in the Lord."*

Fearing God gives you insight into His sovereignty and that makes you *very* secure. Reports of evil deeds or threats will not bring anxiety and hopelessness because you know God will deliver you, and that you are securely in the palm of His hand...even when evil abounds. David had the right attitude about evil. Because he feared God he was able to boldly proclaim:

Even though I walk through the valley of the shadow of death, I fear no evil, for You are with me.

                                                        [Psalm 23:4]

I traveled to Greece shortly after September 11, 2001, the day terrorists attacked the World Trade Center Towers and the Pentagon. Before my trip I received a number of letters from members of my church saying, "Don't go on this trip! It is not safe for you to travel. We love you too much to let you go." One dear woman said, "I want to tie you down. Don't go!" I appreciated those letters because I knew the people who wrote them really cared about me, but I am a Christian! God instructs me to fear *only* Him [Deuteronomy 6:13]. God was in control of my life after September 11th just as He had been *before* that day. I had no reason to fear the future. So I prayed and asked God to speak to me if He didn't want me to go and I would cancel my trip. I went on the trip and everything was fine. If God had allowed me to encounter some difficulty or even tragedy, I know from experience and from the truth of His Word that He would have used it for a good purpose!

> *God causes all things to work together for good to those who love God, to those who are called according to His purpose. [Romans 8:28]*

God holds the future.

There is no greater security than that!

> *Verse 8:*   *"His heart is upheld, he will not fear, until he looks with satisfaction on his adversaries."*

In other words, God will act on your behalf and cause things to work in your favor when you fear Him. He will even take care of those who come up against you.

> *Verse 9:*   *"He has given freely to the poor; His righteousness endures forever; His horn will be exalted in honor."*

When you fear God you choose righteous living. The way in which you live...your righteous acts...will have influence long after you are gone. In the Bible *"horn"* is a symbol of strength. The last phrase in verse 9 essentially says your strength of character will be honored.

Imagine what the American Church would look like if it were filled with men and women who fit the description of Psalm 112. It is not impossible! According to Luke it happened in the early Church after the Holy Spirit was birthed among believers on the day of Pentecost.

> *So the church throughout all Judea and Galilee and Samaria enjoyed peace, being built up; and, going on in the fear of the Lord and in the comfort of the Holy Spirit, it continued to increase. [Acts 9:31]*

If the American Church wants revival...wants God to move among believers and in our cities—*we must fear God!* Only then will He send His Holy Spirit to work in and through us. I have believed for years that if the church would embrace the fear of the Lord it would bring an infusion of forgiveness, holiness, prayer, evangelism, miracles, love and obedience.

Becoming God's Confidant

Psalm 25:14 says:

> *The secret of the LORD is for those who fear him, And He will make them know His covenant.*

I want to be a person God can trust with His secrets! One of my regular prayers is, "Lord I want to fear You! I want godly fear to come into my very being, my bones, my soul, my mind."

When you embrace the fear of God you will begin to manifest the character necessary to bring transformation in your family, church and community. You will become the kind of person God can trust with His secrets!

Fear Is *NOT*...

So what is the fear of the Lord...this discipline that needs to be developed for Christians in the American Church to experience God's favor in every facet of our lives?

Allow me to explain what it is ***not!***

Fear of the Lord is not extreme respect for God. It is not the honor you would show President Bush, the respect you have for a policeman or the reverence that requires you to stand when a judge enters his courtroom.

Fear of the Lord does not involve torment. Some people associate fear with torment because they have been abused. _God is not like that!_ He is not watching and waiting for you to mess up so He can squish you like an ant. When the Bible refers to fearing God it has no association with torment.

Fear Defined

To understand the fear of the Lord it is helpful to know the definition of _"fear."_

> **FEAR** n: an unpleasant, often strong, emotion caused by anticipation or awareness of danger; anxious concern; profound reverence and awe; reasons for alarm.

It is also important to know the meaning of the Hebrew and Greek words used in scripture that are translated "fear" in English. The Hebrew word used most often for "fear" is the Old Testament word _yare_. It is the word used in Deuteronomy 6:13:

> You shall **fear** only the Lord your God; and you shall worship Him and swear by His name.

That word yare is translated _"afraid"_ in Zechariah 9:5. It is used to describe how Israel's enemies felt when they saw God destroy another of Israel's enemies with fire... knowing they were next!

The Hebrew word _yirah_, a form of _yare_, is frequently used when fear of the Lord is associated with benefits such as in these examples from Proverbs:

> The fear of the Lord prolongs life. [10:27]

> In the fear of the Lord there is strong confidence, and His children will have refuge. [14:26]

The reward of humility and the fear of the Lord are riches, honor and life. [22:4]

Though *yirah* is a slight variation of yare, it still simply means *"fear!"*

Pachad is another Hebrew word often translated *"fear."* It means *"alarm; terror; dread."* It is the word used in 2 Chronicles 17:10:

*And the **fear** of the LORD fell upon all the kingdoms of the lands that were round about Judah, so that they made no war against Jehoshaphat. [KJV]*

There are several Greek words for "fear." The two used most often in the New Testament to describe the fear of the Lord are *phobeo* and *phobos*.

Phobeo means *"to frighten or terrify"*; it is the word Jesus used when He said:

*Do not **fear** those who kill the body but are unable to kill the soul; but rather **fear** Him who is able to destroy both soul and body in hell. [Matthew 10:28]*

Phobos, means *"alarm or fright; fear, dread, terror."* Luke used this word to describe the people's response toward God when they saw Jesus heal the paralytic in Luke 5:26:

*They were all struck with astonishment and began glorifying God; and they were filled with **fear**, saying, 'We have seen remarkable things today.'*

Friend, when the Bible says *"fear"* it means fear!

That seems harsh to many, so some try to soften the blow by explaining that it really means honor, respect or reverence.

That is not what scripture says!

If God meant something other than true *fear*, as described by the Hebrew and Greek words used in Scripture, He easily could have inspired Isaiah, Jeremiah, David, Solomon, Malachi, Jesus, John, Peter and Paul to write other words. But these men chose words that mean *fear, alarm, terror and dread.*

Love...Forgiveness...Friendship...FEAR!

Fear of the Lord is so important, yet it is largely ignored by many Christians.

Christians love to talk about the LOVE OF GOD!

That is good...we should talk about it! Three times each weekend I have the privilege of standing alongside my spiritual family of brothers and sisters to worship our Father, experience His love and enjoy His presence. There is nothing better! I sense God's presence more in those surroundings than when I worship alone, and I have a deeper sense of His love for me. It is wonderful!

Christians love to talk about the FORGIVENESS OF GOD!

Forgiveness is one of the greatest benefits of Christianity! Every day you have the opportunity to start with a clean slate. If you blew it yesterday, it is okay! When you truly repent, He forgives you and *forgets* your sin!

Christians love to talk about JESUS OUR FRIEND!

He told us in John 15 that a friend is one who will lay down his life for another and Jesus certainly did that for you and me! Jesus is a friend! But He is also a Lord, King, God and Creator! With one snap of His finger He can turn a person into a piece of dust.

Christians need to talk about the FEAR OF THE LORD!

It is difficult to relate to our loving, kind, merciful God in this way, but look again at Jesus' words in Matthew 10:28. This time I replaced the word *"fear"* with *"be terrified,"* which is the meaning of the word Matthew used which is *"phobeo:"*

*Do not **be terrified by** those who kill the body but are unable to kill the soul; but rather **be terrified of** Him who is able to destroy both soul and body in hell.*

Fear needs to be a Christian's response to God!

It is important to remember that when I insert the word terrified it does not mean terrified by fear of torment or torture. Paul says in Romans 11:22:

Behold then the kindness and severity of God; to those who fell, severity, but to you, God's kindness.

God is severe...He must be taken seriously. But more than severe, He is kind and good. He repeatedly extends opportunities for His children to escape severity when they choose to obey.

The Fear of the Lord Defined

After much thought and prayer I can come to believe that the fear of the Lord is comprised of two truths:

1. An understanding that there are consequences for disobedience and blessings for obedience.

2. A growing awareness of who God is as we see the first truth played out in our lives or others'.

Consequences for Disobeying God

The American Church has largely forgotten that there are real consequences for disobeying God. The Nation certainly does not believe it! Consequences are evident everywhere, but for some reason people...including Christians...don't make the connection between disobedience and consequence. This may be in part due to the microwave, instant access, ATM mentality of society. We expect everything to be instantaneous, but consequences for disobedience are not always immediate. As a result, people wrongly believe that there are no consequences for sin!

As it says in Ecclesiastes 8:11:

Because the sentence against an evil deed is not executed

quickly, therefore the hearts of the sons of men among them are given fully to do evil.

The world is filled with people, both in and out of the Church who have embraced sin and compromise and are not seemingly suffering any consequences. They do not see any consequences, and so they assume there are none! The truth is...many of the consequences come later in life, and those that are immediate are not necessarily visible in the short term (example STDs).

Sowing and Reaping

American Christians think they can get around the rules and not really suffer for their choices. They could not be more wrong. People sow what they reap!

Do not be deceived, God is not mocked; for whatever a man sows, this he also will reap. [Galatians 6:7]

I am teaching my children that there are consequences for disobedience. Sometimes that consequence is a spanking. As a result, my children fear me. My children do not obey me out of "honor, respect and reverence." It is out of "fear and dread" of what will happen if they do not obey! Understand, I do not beat my children! I do not strike them in anger. Their fear is not fear of torment or torture. They know I love them and it is because I love them that I lovingly spank them. The fear they have of me is beneficial to them. It teaches them to respect my boundaries so when they grow up they will respect society's boundaries and God's boundaries,

There is a generation of young people who need to learn to fear authority. That fear is almost absent in America. I want my kids to know that when they buck authority...when they disobey my wife, Mary, or me...there is a consequence. _Not_ teaching them about consequences would be cruel! They would suffer for it dearly as adults. There are scores of young people today who are walking testimonies of this truth.

To teach my children the valuable lesson of consequences for disobedience we have "the spanking stick."

When there is a need for a spanking…a consequence for their behavior, I march them into the room to administer their due punishment with a resolution of steel! Then I catch a glimpse of "those precious eyes." My resolve suddenly crumbles, and in the recesses of my heart I cry out for God to give me the strength to do my duty. It is hard to discipline our children, but it must be done for the sake of their souls!

No Fear? *No Love!*

There are those who would say, "I'm sorry Dave, but I can't comprehend fearing God. He is my friend! I love Him. He's my Abba Father and He loves me." Friend, allow me to share a harsh truth with you: if you do not fear God you do not love Him! It is impossible. Jesus said:

If you love me you will keep my commandments.
[John 14:15]

It is the fear of God that motivates obedience to His commandments. You cannot love God unless you fear Him.

Fear and Appreciation

The second aspect of fearing God is growing in appreciation of God and His character. The Bible instructs you to stand in awe of God because of His power, ability and character.

You who fear the Lord praise Him. All you descendants of Jacob glorify Him and stand in awe of Him all you descendants of Israel. [Psalm 22:23]

Let all the earth fear the Lord, let all the inhabitants of the world stand in awe of Him. [Psalm 33:8]

Unfortunately, many people disregard God because they do not understand Him. Ironically, that is the very reason they should be in awe of Him. No one can understand God or His ways. He is far too great to comprehend. Personally, that makes me feel secure! If I could understand God…predict His actions…know His thoughts, I would be His equal. That would make Him much too small to teach me, guide me, protect and perfect me.

I need a God who is immense!

I need a God who knows immeasurably more than I will ever know...whose power is beyond my comprehension and whose ways are superior to my own. That I cannot understand Him inspires me to have fearful reverence for Him!

God is a Paradox

Still, it is understandable that many people are confused about God's character. God is a paradox, having seemingly contradictory qualities. Prophetic author and speaker Graham Cooke defines paradox as *"two opposites contained within the same truth."* That certainly describes God! He is holy and intolerant of sin, while at the same time merciful and forgiving of sin. These are opposite traits both contained in the true character of God.

Predestination offers another example of seeming contradiction. Scripture states that God preordained everything, *and* that He allows humans to have free will. How can this be? It does not seem possible. It is logical that predestination and free will cannot co-exist. But both are true because the Bible states them as fact. You must simply accept them in faith. As you do, you will grow in appreciation of God and His character.

Fear Transforms

My children's fear of me began as true fear: dread and terror. But as that fear transforms who they are, it begins to change into respect, honor and reverence. My fear of the Lord has gone through changes too, and I have come to know Him well enough to respect, honor and reverence His heart of goodness, and love as much as I fear and dread His hand of discipline.

As you read this book you will develop a clearer understanding of what it means to fear the Lord. You will learn how to begin fearing Him and how to apply that fear in your marriage, church, finances, business and with your children. You will learn why God desires that you fear Him; you will grow in appreciation of your Savior, the One who is able to deliver and heal you. I can guarantee with confidence that if you will learn to fear the Lord, you will develop a deeper love for the One who is able to rend the heavens, come down and do miracles in your heart, your home and your city.

The more you fear and appreciate God, the more trust and faith you have that He can do mighty things.

Fear God and be blessed!

CHAPTER TWO

The Fear of the Lord:
Blessing or Consequence?

O fear the Lord, you His saints; For to those who fear Him there is no want. (Psalm 34:9)

There is only one thing that brings the blessing of God on your life: obedience! God loves you, has great plans for you and deeply desires to bless you. You provide Him with the opportunity when you choose to fear Him and obey Him. If, however, you disobey God and pursue your own desires, God's desire to bless you does not change...but the degree and delivery of blessing on your life will definitely change.

Disobedience forces God to allow you to experience the consequences of your decision to disobey. Often, these consequences are quite effective in drawing us back to God. Pain has an amazing ability to teach the fear of the Lord!

Early Choices Set Lifelong Courses

Fearing the Lord is a choice; we all have that choice.

You can be saved, a heaven bound Christian, and still choose *not* to fear God. You will not sacrifice salvation, but as long as you are living in disobedience you will give up the blessings that come from fearing God...blessings like peace, joy, satisfaction, and success are reserved for people who choose to fear Him.

My brother Mark and I, supported by our staff and church members, are deeply committed to young people. We offer extensive programs for teens and young adults because we want to provide godly options and opportunities to them at an age when Satan's lures are strongest. People begin making choices at age 12 or 13 that will impact their lives for many years. We hope to encourage them at a young age to plot a course God can bless by helping them see the value of fearing the Lord.

My personal commitment to support children and youth ministry comes from my sincere desire to spare others the pain I suffered. When I was about 12 or 13 years old I decided that church was an impediment to having fun. It seemed God had rules forbidding everything that interested me! They seemed antiquated...just like the people who went to church. I thought, "The Bible was written so long ago it has nothing to do with life today. And the people at church seem so out of touch with the *real* world!" So I made a choice to go my own way...I wanted nothing to do with God! That <u>one</u> decision bred destruction in almost every area of my life and nearly resulted in my death.

Approximately nine years after I rejected God and church I was under the care of a psychiatrist. I had taken so many drugs and probably killed so many brain cells that I had lost the ability to think normally. Doctors could not help me beyond prescribing drugs to sedate me. When I was not on medication I was afraid of everything! I was a mess...the consequence for choosing to disobey God.

The Blessing of Obedience

Genesis 22 offers one of history's most provocative accounts of someone who understood the fear of the Lord and chose obedience. God instructed Abraham to build an altar, and then sacrifice his only son, Isaac, as a burnt offering.

I am a father with only one son. I cannot imagine how I would respond if God commanded me to hand over my son to be sacrificed. It is unthinkable to consider thrusting a knife in his chest and torching him myself!

Abraham feared God and chose to obey Him, so father and son set off for Mount Moriah, the place where God said Abraham was to make the sacrifice. At some point on their trek up the hill Isaac noticed they brought all the instruments for a sacrifice except the lamb. He asked his father about it, and Abraham explained that

God would provide a lamb for the offering. When they reached the top of the hill Abraham built an altar and placed the wood on top of it.

I believe that once the altar was built Abraham acted quickly. He did not want his son to suffer...either from a wound that was not instantly fatal or from lying there for any length of time knowing what his father was about to do.

Abraham quickly bound Isaac and laid him on top of the wood.

With one swift motion Abraham raised the sharp dagger directly above Isaac's heart, but in the instant before the blade plunged downward, Abraham was stopped by a voice from heaven:

> *But the angel of the Lord called to him from heaven and said, "Abraham, Abraham!" And he said, "Here I am." He said, "Do not stretch out your hand against the lad, and do nothing to him; for now I know that you fear God, since you have not withheld your son, your only son, from Me." [Genesis 22:11-12]*

Fearing God is recognizing that all you have is His to take. You can be certain that if God asks you to give up anything He has good reason. He is a loving Father who does not issue commands to deprive or oppress you, but to protect and bless you. In fact, His boundaries are meant to prevent suffering. Consequences for disobedience usually are the natural repercussions from destructive behavior (not punishment implemented by God).

Obedience Is Better Than Sacrifice

Imagine with me for a moment just some of the rationalizations Abraham could have chosen instead of obedience!

"Lord, Isaac is my only son! If I kill him there is no heir to Your promise and this entire tribe will be in turmoil. What will my wife say? Worse yet, what will she do?"

"Lord, I know You said to offer Isaac as a sacrifice... and I will offer a sacrifice...but Isaac was a gift, a promise from You! Surely You are not the kind of God who would take back a gift."

"God, I will buy the most expensive ram I can find. I'll put gold on its horns and carry it all the way up to the top of that mountain and sacrifice it to You. It will be the best, most extravagant sacrifice You ever received!"

Sacrifice was not what God wanted from Abraham...He wanted obedience! Obedience is always God's preferred form of worship from His people:

> Has the Lord as much delight in burnt offerings and sacrifices as in obeying the voice of the Lord? Behold, **to obey is better than sacrifice**, and to heed than the fat of rams. [1 Samuel 15:22]

Abraham's obedience resulted in a blessing for you and me! God promised to bless *all peoples* on earth through Abraham [Genesis 12:8]. Isaac was the father of Jacob (or Israel), and Jacob was the father of Judah. Jesus was a descendant of Judah; so when He redeemed all mankind on the cross, God's promise was fulfilled...*all peoples* on earth were blessed through Abraham! When you and I put our faith in Jesus we became children of Abraham [Romans 9; Galatians 3:7-9 & 29]!

Fearing God More Than Man

Some believers face a difficult test when they are forced to choose between obeying God and man. The one who fears God knows that the best option...the blessed option...is obeying God.

Several hundred years after Abraham died, his descendants, the Israelites, were living in Egypt. The family had grown to great numbers and the Egyptians began to feel threatened. Pharaoh feared that the Israelites might rise up against him so he forced them into slavery, but the more the Israelites were afflicted, the more they multiplied. Pharaoh devised a plan to stop Israel's growth, but it also failed because the midwives he commanded to help him feared God more than man:

> Then the king of Egypt spoke to the Hebrew midwives, one of whom was named Shiphrah and the other was named Puah; and he said, "When you are helping the Hebrew

*women to give birth and see them upon the birthstool, if it is a son, then you shall put him to death; but if it is a daughter, then she shall live. **But the midwives feared God**, and did not do as the king of Egypt had commanded them, but let the boys live. So the king of Egypt called for the midwives and said to them, "Why have you done this thing, and let the boys live?" The midwives said to Pharaoh, "Because the Hebrew women are not as the Egyptian women; for they are vigorous and give birth before the midwife can get to them." So God was good to the midwives, and the people multiplied, and became very mighty. [Exodus 1:15-20]*

The midwives understood that God is a higher authority than Pharaoh, and chose to obey Him. God responded by blessing them! Verse 21 says He established households for them...God gave them secure, stable homes.

You who fear the Lord, trust in the Lord; He is their help and their shield. [Psalm 115:11]

It is amazing to see what God will do on behalf of those who fear Him. These women deliberately disobeyed Pharaoh and he knew it...he was not stupid! It was not logical to think that every pregnant Israelite woman gave birth before a midwife could arrive. Certainly there were more than two Hebrew midwives for thousands of Israelite women. The two named in scripture were obviously the head midwives. Pharaoh had the power to kill the midwives for defying his authority, but he did not...God protected them!

The Blessing of Provision

The Bible says those who make a choice to fear God and obey Him will be blessed:

O fear the Lord, you His saints; for to those who fear Him there is no want. [Psalm 34:9]

If you make the decision to obey God and live by biblical principles, He will provide everything you need.

I had the privilege of witnessing a wonderful testimony of God's provision during my first mission trip to Cuba a few years ago. I was having dinner with a Cuban doctor and her husband. They ordered steak...the first meat they had eaten in several months. In Cuba, people do not buy food whenever they need it like we do in the United States. Food is allocated to families once a month by the Cuban government. Each family receives one sack of potatoes, one chicken, some rice and a few staples...not nearly enough food for a family to survive.

There is a hidden economy, but food purchased on the black market is very expensive. I had seen the couple's tiny home and knew that a doctor's salary was a mere $60.00 per month. "How do you survive?" I asked, "especially working for the church? The church is too poor to give you a salary, so how in the world do you feed your family and pay bills?" The doctor replied, "There are many days where I wake up in the morning knowing there is not enough food for my children, let alone for my husband and myself. I don't know how I am going to feed them, but somehow by the time we go to bed at night everyone has eaten. That is our testimony and that is the testimony of every Christian family in Cuba."

They may have eaten only rice, beans or apples, but God provided for them...every day God miraculously feeds His Cuban children!

He will bless those who fear the Lord, the small together with the great. [Psalm 115:13]

God's people in Cuba are truly blessed. They do not have the material blessings we often take for granted in the United States, but they receive spiritual blessings many Americans and American churches will never know!

The Promise of Prosperity

There are wonderful promises in the Bible for the person who chooses to fear the Lord.

So that you and your son and your grandson might fear the Lord your God, to keep all His statutes and His commandments which I command you, all the days of your life, and that your days may be prolonged.

[Deuteronomy 6:2]

If you take God seriously and obey His Word, you will live longer! That is what this scripture in Deuteronomy says...and from Proverbs you see that it is not only a long life, but a peaceful one.

The fear of the Lord is a fountain of life, that one may avoid the snares of death. [Proverbs 14:27]

The fear of the Lord leads to life. So that one may sleep satisfied, untouched by evil. [Proverbs 19:23]

In the fear of the Lord there is strong confidence, and his children will have refuge. [Proverbs 14:26]

When you fear the Lord there is no need to fear anything or anyone else! His protection and faithfulness time and time again will assure you that He can be trusted in any situation. You will grow to be confident in Him and live a life free from fear.

The reward of humility and the fear of the Lord are riches, honor and life. [Proverbs 22:4]

God's favor is on those who fear Him!

The Cuban Christians do not live in conditions most of us would consider satisfactory, but in their society they are better off than the average Cuban. God's favor is not measured in material things, but in true *prosperity*...peace, contentment, safety, provision and right relationship with God and man. All these blessings are promised in scripture to those who fear the Lord.

Blessing in Tribulation

Sometimes God's people suffer even though they fear the Lord. Christians all around the world who have chosen to obey God are imprisoned or killed. Scripture says they are blessed:

If you are reviled for the name of Christ, you are blessed, because the Spirit of glory and of God rests on you.
[1 Peter 4:14]

When someone is persecuted or martyred for their faith in God, He gives them supernatural courage, strength, and peace. Countless Christians throughout history have withstood horrendous, even torturous ordeals, refusing to renounce Christ or disobey God knowing that doing so would have spared them.

Even in America Christians sometimes suffer discrimination for choosing to obey God. Christian students are ridiculed for their stand on purity and prayer. In the workplace Christians are often treated with contempt because of their beliefs against abortion, homosexuality and other culturally popular, sinful lifestyles.

Obeying God is not always easy, <u>but it is always right</u>!

Floods, Fire and Twenty-First Century Salt

The Old Testament conveys basically two messages: the promises of the coming Messiah and a record of how God deals with His people.

Today when Christians choose to rationalize and justify disobedience, God does not respond, as in ancient times, by flooding the Earth, sending hailstorms of fire and brimstone, or turning people into pillars of salt. Essentially He says, "Okay! Go your way, but you will suffer the consequences of that decision."

The first and worst consequence of disobedience is a broken relationship with God.

Many Christians believe they can live a compromised life and still enjoy fellowship with Him. It does not work that way. God promised never to leave nor forsake His people, and He does not! But our relationship with Him...sensing and enjoying His presence, walking in His power and receiving guidance...is stifled by sin.

In my first book, *Prayer Will Change Your World,* I give an in-depth explanation of the five hindrances to prayer. Number one on the list is sin! When you permit sin in your life your prayers are hindered before God.

Some people believe they are the exception and their compromise will not affect their relationship with God. I am especially astonished by one rationalization I hear all the time: "I know scripture says I should not marry a non-Christian, but God has given me permission to do it! He brought this person into my life and I believe He wants us to be together." I was shocked when one woman added, "This man is my savior." Oh, no he is not!

Whatever the cost for obeying God, generally it is small in comparison to the price you pay for disobedience. The emotional pain of relinquishing an ungodly relationship is nothing compared to the agonizing consequences for being involved in one.

Still, far too many Christians in America think they can disobey God and escape the consequences. It is my sincere hope and prayer that we are living in a time when that philosophy is being stripped away. Hopefully people will begin to reject their propensity to rationalize and justify sin. The real and devastating consequences for sin in our society are so evident that even non-believers are beginning to recognize them.

Cheap Grace

The attitude that allows a believer to say, "I am going to sin but God will forgive me" is called *cheap grace*. It is what prompted Martin Luther to author the 95 Theses in 1492...a list of 95 things *wrong* with the Catholic Church.

One day Luther, a Catholic priest, encountered a drunken parishioner. When Luther confronted the man he said, "It doesn't matter what I do because God forgives me!" and handed Luther a sheet of paper called an "indulgence"...a note of forgiveness for all sorts of sins.

A priest named Johann Tetzel, with the blessing of the Catholic Church, was *selling* "indulgences" which were valid for certain periods of time: forty days, eighty days or one year. The funds collected were used to build Saint Peter's Cathedral in Rome.

Luther was appalled! His objection to cheap grace and commitment to forgiveness through repentance was heresy to the Catholic Church and resulted in his excommunication.

Some people today cling to the brand of cheap grace that angered Luther. They see God's merciful, forgiving character as something of a religious "get out of jail free" card. They feel the liberty to sin as long as they confess it and ask forgiveness. They think doing so obligates God to forgive them and cancel the consequences.

Not so!

God forgives those who are repentant, but confession alone is not repentance! Repentance means there must be a change of heart...a genuine desire to turn away from sinful behavior with the intention never to return. If a repentant person could turn back the clock, they would choose not to sin.

Praise the Lord that when you truly repent the Lord forgives you and forgets your sin.

For I will be merciful to their iniquities, and I will remember their sins no more. [Hebrews 8:12]

I am happy to tell you, the grace of God covers your sin and acts as a balm for your wounded spirit when you are truly repentant. But there is nothing cheap about it! It cost God His only Son Jesus' life.

Miraculous Mercy

Though there are always consequences for sin, sometimes God chooses to ease or remove them. Many years ago I was dying from a drug overdose...I repented for my sinful living and God miraculously healed me. His powerful presence was so strong that a young man who was next to me was also deeply affected. I did not deserve healing, and the other man did not even ask to experience God's presence...but that's the miraculous mercy of God.

I did suffer other consequences because of my sin, but was spared the consequence of death. Why God allows some consequences and covers others by His mercy is a mystery that only He understands.

Consequences: A Reforming Influence

One thing I have come to understand is that sin devastates lives. As a pastor, I see the consequences of disobedience and sin almost daily. I see pain, sorrow, loss, depression, loneliness, guilt, anger, bitterness and more. Christians who should know better choose to disobey God. His warnings about the destructive power of sin are to *protect* His people from pain. Instead, they choose to sin and then blame Him for their suffering.

I will never forget an incident that opened my eyes and changed my heart forever.

I had been a Christian for only a short time. I was hungry for God and wanted to spend every waking moment in church. I drove a couple of hours from my home in San Diego to the Anaheim Vineyard to participate in fantastic worship and hear John Wimber speak. Unfortunately, I was still justifying and rationalizing a lot of sin in my life, especially a wrong relationship. I would tell myself, "God understands that I am only human," then I would tell Him, "Lord, You know that I'd like to obey You but I just can't. Besides, after everything I have done, this cannot be *that* bad."

I was in the service with my hands raised, worshipping God and sensing His presence, when suddenly God spoke very clearly to me and said, "If you continue in this compromising sin there will be consequences." I stopped, dropped my hands to my side, opened my eyes and said, "Consequences?"

God certainly had my attention!

The last thing on earth I needed more of was more consequences! As the result of my indulgent living I had already literally lost my mind and was seeing a psychiatrist. I said, "Lord, I have suffered enough consequences and have wasted too much of my life. I do not know how many years it will take to straighten out my mind so I can attempt to live a normal life, but I know for certain I do not want any more consequences!"

Friend, that is genuine, life-reforming fear of the Lord. At that very moment I made a decision to obey God simply because I was afraid of what might happen if I did not! I have never regretted my choice...in the years since, my commitment to fear the Lord has only grown stronger.

My resolve is bolstered as I see consequences for disobedience manifested in the lives of some of the people I pastor. I know many of the intimate details of their choices and I see time and time again that disobedience carries a high price. That alone has kept me safely in the fear of the Lord.

Your Sin Will Find You Out

The Bible says teachers are judged more strictly than other believers [James 3:1], and I think it is partly because we so frequently see the result of sin. There is no excuse for disobedience from someone like me who knows the truth of God's Word...both from studying it myself and from seeing the results in people's lives.

Sin will always finds you out, whether you are a pastor, or an unbeliever! The Word of God declares it!

Behold, you have sinned against the Lord, and be sure your sin will find you out. [Numbers 32:23]

Our sins testify against us. [Isaiah 59:12]

I know Christians who have married unbelievers or cultivated friendships that pulled them away from God. I have heard every excuse imaginable for financial unfaithfulness and have watched Christians cling to wrong behavior because of pride and stubbornness. I have seen lifelong believers compromise honesty and integrity for personal gain...making idols of money, prestige and career. Some neglect their marriage responsibilities while others, especially young people, experiment with things they should never consider.

I know all too well the consequences that result from disobeying God: bitterness and anger in marriages, loneliness and broken homes, rebellious children, wasted lives, depression, addiction, disease, lack of purpose, alienation, untimely death, damaged health and every emotional bondage imaginable. All these things could be avoided if God's people would listen to His Word!

The Blessing of Beginning Young

The younger you are, the more important it is for you to heed this warning and fear God! If you are a young man or woman, and make a choice now to fear God, you will never be sorry. You will set yourself on a course to enjoy a happy marriage and be successful in every aspect of life.

I wanted a wife and children like most young men, but because of consequences for my choices I did not marry until later in life. I was 40 years old before I finally had the 1st of three children.

My younger brother, John, was not like me. He did his best to obey God in every way. John is in his early thirties now and has a great family and ministry. Many of God's blessings have come to him 15 years earlier than I received them, because early in his life he made a choice to fear God. God has given me a wonderful family, but I will never reclaim my lost years. John does not have lost years to regret!

A Harvest of Heartaches

Some people live in the delusion that they can compromise God's Word without repercussions because they do not suffer immediate consequences. They could not be more wrong. While some consequences for sin are immediately evident, often they do not materialize until much later. One thing is certain, however, the consequences will come.

Do not be deceived, God is not mocked; for whatever a man sows, this he will also reap. [Galatians 6:7]

Because the sentence against an evil deed is not executed quickly, therefore the hearts of the sons of men among them are given fully to do evil. [Ecclesiastes 8:11]

God is not anxiously waiting for people to do something wrong so He can punish them. He weeps over sin and the suffering of His people. He chose to suffer the ultimate consequence for sin Himself...death! But when you disobey God there is a sentence on your life: it may take five, ten, even fifteen years, but as sure as the sun rises in the East and sets in the West, your season of sowing sin will reap a heartbreaking harvest of consequences.

A Bad Beginning

Know from Proverbs chapter 1 that fearing the Lord is the beginning of knowledge, understanding and wisdom. Refusing to fear Him is also a beginning...the beginning of a long, hard road of separation between an individual and God.

> *Then they will call on Me, but I will not answer; they will seek Me diligently, but they will not find Me, because they hated knowledge and did not choose the fear of the Lord.*
> *[Proverbs 1:28-29]*

It is clear that this scripture speaks specifically of Christians because it is about people who are seeking Him diligently. Today they are the people who attend church, read the Bible regularly and pray. Proverbs says they do not find Him because they hate knowledge and refuse to fear Him. When they make choices contrary to God's directives they are essentially saying, "I reject Your knowledge, God! I am not going to accept what You say about this issue, instead I will follow my own counsel." Their minds and mouths may not say it, but their actions do.

That is what the Bible calls *hating knowledge.*

> *They would not accept My counsel, they spurned all of My reproof. So they shall eat of the fruit of their own way and be satiated with their own devices. For the waywardness of the naive shall kill them, and the complacency of fools shall destroy them. But he who listens to me shall live securely, and shall be at ease from the dread of evil.*
> *[Proverbs 1:30-33]*

Notice God's response. He steps back and basically says, "Beloved, My desire is to bless you but if you insist on disobedience

I will allow you to pursue your desires and learn the hard way." According to Scripture, death and destruction will be the result; it could be literal or it could be the death and destruction of blessings...purity, peace, relationships, finances and health. In either case, refusing God's counsel is the beginning of a journey you will eventually regret.

I have a special word of warning for young people who disobey God: if you have parents who pray for you, the odds are stacked against you...you might as well give up now because you *will* return to God. Sooner or later you are going to reap the consequences: fail at a marriage or two, succumb to health problems or suffer financial disaster. Eventually, you will come back to God because He *loves* to bless praying parents. You are better off saving yourself the trouble by surrendering now.

Consequences: A Valuable Tool

Consequences can be a valuable tool in the hand of God. The pain inflicted by the sharp edge of consequence is one reason many wayward Christians rethink their rebellion and return to God.

Consequences also can be a useful tool in the hand of a repentant Christian. I know a man who made some wrong decisions; he had been married three times and suffered many consequences. Though he could not reclaim his wasted years, he found a way to make the experience beneficial. As often as the Lord gives him opportunity, he shares his testimony with men having marriage problems. Those who heed his warning have the opportunity to learn from his pain instead of suffering their own.

A person who fears God is rewarded with wisdom, which manifests itself as the fruits of the Spirit: love, joy, peace, patience, kindness, goodness, faithfulness, gentleness and self-control [Galatians 5:22].

A person does not have to be repentant, however, for the consequences they reap from disobedience to be a valuable teaching tool to others. The biblical account of Ananias and Sapphira in Acts 5 offers a good example of this truth.

Ananias and his wife, Sapphira, lied to the Apostle Peter and to God about the amount of money they received for selling their property. Both of them dropped dead that very day! Imagine your response if you witnessed the event! Even if you never had been tempted to do as they did, you would likely be on your face begging God's forgiveness for something you had done.

That, my friend, is a good, healthy fear of the Lord!

The Desperately Sick Heart

Satan frequently tries to convince believers that compromising God's Word is the only way to experience the desires of their heart: marriage, a home, fun, success. He does not have to work very hard because the human heart is deceitful, sick and selfish:

The heart is more deceitful than all else and is desperately sick; who can understand it? [Jeremiah 17:9]

If you think God is telling you it is okay for you to marry a non-Christian you are *not* hearing from God!

If you think God will permit you to have sex outside of marriage, lie on your tax returns, get drunk, or hold a grudge, you are not listening to the Lord!

God never contradicts His Word.

In truth, you are listening to the devil, your own sick heart, or both.

Friend, our hearts are wicked and cannot be trusted. I know! Every time I have followed my heart instead of God's Word the result has always been heartache.

There is a way which seems right to a man, but its end is the way of death. [Proverbs 14:12]

Our minds often mislead us too!

When you are faced with the dilemma of following logic or God's Word, run as quickly as you can to obey God's Word regardless of how illogical it may seem. Logic can be a huge, destructive idol.

Fear the Lord in Temptation

When you say "no" to temptation, God is able to bless you abundantly; just look at the life of Joseph [Genesis 39-41]! There is no doubt in my mind that Potipher's wife was a very beautiful woman and her efforts to seduce Joseph were very appealing. Joseph, however, feared God...he had wisdom and discernment from God...so when he was cornered by temptation Joseph ran! His response brought tribulation for a season but ultimately he was exalted for it. Pharaoh promoted Joseph to rule over Egypt because Joseph had great wisdom and discernment from God [Genesis 41:39-45].

Seek First His Kingdom and His Righteousness

Jesus said the key to receiving the desires of your heart is not seeking them, but seeking God's Kingdom and righteousness:

For this reason I say to you, do not be anxious for your life, as to what you shall eat, or what you shall drink; nor for your body, as to what you shall put on. Is not life more than food, and the body than clothing? But seek first His kingdom and His righteousness, and all these things will be added to you. [Matthew 6:25 and 33]

When you fear God, His Kingdom and righteousness become your priority...and your material and emotional needs become His priority.

Psalm 25:14 says:

The secret of the LORD is for those who fear Him, and He will make them know His covenant.

Every day I ask God to increase my ability to fear Him because I want to know His secrets! Those secrets contained in God's Word will help me know how to be a good husband and father, bring direction to my life, success to my ministry, and enable me to live a life rich with the fruits of the Spirit. Not everyone has access to those secrets...they are reserved for those who choose to fear Him.

Fearing the Lord is my choice and I pray it will be yours too. May we all be filled with the fear that produces blessing until Jesus returns!

CHAPTER THREE

Fear That Produces an Appreciation of God

By the word of the Lord the heavens were made, and by the breath of His mouth all their host. He gathers the waters of the sea together as a heap; He lays up the deeps in storehouses. Let all the earth fear the Lord; Let all the inhabitants of the world stand in awe of Him.

[Psalm 33:6-8]

What image comes to your mind when you think of God? I do not mean Jesus. It is relatively easy to imagine our Savior in human form...teaching the multitudes, reclining at the Passover table or expiring on the cross. It is quite different to picture the glorious, majestic, Almighty God...in fact I personally do not think it is possible. If you try, two things are certain to happen: you will have a greater appreciation of God and your fear of Him will increase.

Consider for a moment the God who created molten lava and the delicate tissue of your eardrum...towering sequoias and the tiny pollen-collecting hairs on a honeybee. Fixing your mind on creation inspires awe for the Creator, but try conjuring up His image and you will always come up short.

Indescribable Images

After receiving visions of God, Ezekiel and the Apostle John struggled to describe what they saw. That is evident from the things they wrote regarding His face and form. Here are a few of their descriptions as recorded in the books of Ezekiel and Revelation:

- like jasper stone and sardius in appearance

- a face like the sun shining in its strength

- eyes that are like flames of fire

- a figure with the appearance of a man who is like glowing metal that

- looks like fire from the loin up and something like fire from the loin down

- a radiance all around Him similar to a rainbow

Now close your eyes for a moment and try to picture what you just read. Are you able to visualize Him? Of course you are not! What is described is completely and supernaturally beyond human comprehension.

I have never seen art that depicts God as described by Ezekiel and John. The reason is simple: an artist needs a point of reference to create an image and with God there is none!

To paint a picture of an apple, an artist must have seen an apple at some time in his life. He may creatively interpret the size, shape, and color in his artwork, but because he has a point of reference, the subject of his painting is clear. An artist who has never seen the fruit would have difficulty painting the picture. If something as simple as an apple is hard to paint without a point of reference, you can be certain that it is impossible when the subject is the indescribably magnificent Almighty God!

Like the Appearance of Something Resembling What You Have Never Seen

God exists in a form, time and space beyond human comprehension. That is why the prophet and the apostle struggled to describe Him and those around His throne. Notice in the following text how many times the two men used "like," "something like," "resembled," "resembling," "in appearance" and "the appearance of":

Ezekiel's Description in Ezekiel 1:22-28:

Now over the heads of the living beings [Read Ezekiel 1:1-21 for the prophet's description of the four living creatures and compare it with the Apostle John's description in Revelation 4, reprinted in this chapter] *there was <u>something like</u> an expanse, <u>like</u> the awesome gleam of crystal, spread out over their heads. Under the expanse their wings were stretched out straight, one toward the other; each one also had two wings covering its body on the one side and on the other. I also heard the sound of their wings <u>like</u> the sound of abundant waters as they went, <u>like</u> the voice of the Almighty, a sound of tumult <u>like</u> the sound of an army camp; whenever they stood still, they dropped their wings. And there came a voice from above the expanse that was over their heads; whenever they stood still, they dropped their wings. Now above the expanse that was over their heads there was something <u>resembling</u> a throne, <u>like</u> lapis lazuli <u>in appearance</u>; and on that which <u>resembled</u> a throne, high up, was a figure with <u>the appearance of</u> a man. Then I noticed from <u>the appearance of</u> His loins and upward <u>something like</u> glowing metal that looked <u>like</u> fire all around within it, and from <u>the appearance of</u> His loins and downward I saw <u>something like</u> fire; and there was a radiance around Him. As <u>the appearance of</u> the rainbow in the clouds on a rainy day, so was <u>the appearance of</u> the surrounding radiance. Such was <u>the appearance of</u> the likeness of the glory of the LORD. And when I saw it, I fell on my face and heard a voice speaking."*

John's Description in Revelation 4

After these things I looked, and behold, a door standing open in heaven, and the first voice which I had heard, <u>like</u> the sound of a trumpet speaking with me, said, 'Come up here, and I will show you what must take place after these things.' Immediately I was in the Spirit; and behold, a throne was standing in heaven, and One sitting on the throne. And He who was sitting was <u>like</u> a jasper stone *and a sardius in appearance; and there was a rainbow around the throne, like an emerald in appearance. And around the throne were twenty-four thrones; and upon the thrones I saw twenty-four elders sitting, clothed in white garments, and golden crowns on their heads.*

Out from the throne came flashes of lightning and sounds and peals of thunder. And there were seven lamps of fire burning before the throne, which are the seven Spirits of God [The Seven Spirits of God are listed in Isaiah 11:2]; *and before the throne there was something like a sea of glass, like crystal; and in the center and around the throne, four living creatures full of eyes in front and behind. The first creature was like a lion, and the second creature like a calf, and the third creature had a face like that of a man, and the fourth creature was like a flying eagle. And the four living creatures, each one of them having six wings, are full of eyes around and within; and day and night they do not cease to say, 'HOLY, HOLY, HOLY, is THE LORD GOD, THE ALMIGHTY, WHO WAS AND WHO IS AND WHO IS TO COME.' And when the living creatures give glory and honor and thanks to Him who sits on the throne, to Him who lives forever and ever, the twenty-four elders will fall down before Him who sits on the throne, and will worship Him who lives forever and ever, and will cast their crowns before the throne, saying, 'Worthy are You, our Lord and our God, to receive glory and honor and power; for You created all things, and because of Your will they existed, and were created.'"*

Ezekiel and the Apostle John saw similar visions of God, yet both struggled to find adequate words to describe Him.

Both men refer to crystal and rainbows. Ezekiel describes fiery, glowing metal and John uses gem-like references. Jasper is a clear, emerald green stone and sardius is a stone that appears to be red in direct light but is orange and brown in reflective light. Even with all this detail, I am at a complete loss to imagine the appearance of God.

Ezekiel saw only a glimpse of the Lord and was compelled to fall on his face...it was all his mind could handle. John had a similar response when he saw the resurrected Christ [Revelation 1:17]. I believe people fall on their faces before God because no other response is possible! He is more splendid than any human can comprehend. Even today falling prostrate is a typical response among those who experience the powerful presence of God.

Extraordinary Escorts

Almost as impossible as picturing God is envisioning those surrounding His throne. John described creatures with faces you can easily imagine...a lion, a calf, a man and an eagle...but when he writes that they are covered with eyes, the images blur and evaporate! We simply have no point of reference to picture these creatures.

Ezekiel 1:1-21 describes similar beings but says the eyes cover the wheels next to each creature. I have read these verses more times than I can tell you, yet it remains as great a mystery to me as it was on my first reading.

Eternal Adoration

The twenty-four elders are another enigma. Much is written about them in commentaries, but it is all theory. No one really knows the identity of these elders and why they are at God's throne.

Author, speaker and worship leader Joseph Garlington elaborates on these verses in a way I really appreciate. He says the elders come before the throne of God saying, "Worthy art thou, O Lord our God, to receive glory and honor," and as they cast their eyes upward they get a tiny glimpse of God in all His glory. They scream, fall face down and say, "O God, You are so great! Here is my crown. You can have it!"

The elders lie there breathless for a time, but when they are finally able to speak, they say, "Let's do that again!" They place their crowns on their heads, peek at God, scream, fall to the floor and cast their crowns down at His feet. The elders do this over and over, never growing weary of the ritual, because each time they see a new and different facet of God's glory.

Though we cannot imagine the appearance of God, we can appreciate certain things about Him...and that produces fear of the Lord. Fear of the Lord increases our appreciation of Him and a wonderful circle of worship is perpetuated!

The Troubling Truth About the Trinity

God's appearance is not the only concept that boggles our human minds—many of His other traits are simply beyond comprehension. The trinity is one example.

We worship a triune God—one God consisting of three persons: Father, Son and Holy Spirit. How is one God three individuals? There is no answer that satisfies.

To bring a degree of understanding to the trinity, some scholars compare God's three-in-one nature to water—it can be a gas [steam], a liquid [water] and a solid [ice]. One glaring problem with this analogy is that water is not a gas, liquid and solid all at the same time, while God is simultaneously Father, Son and Holy Spirit!

Scripture says it is impossible to please God without faith; the trinity is one of the scriptural truths that provide us with the opportunity to believe *in faith* and please God.

I Need a BIG God

My inability to understand God is actually a comfort to me. As one pastor put it, "If God were small enough for our minds He would not be big enough for our needs."

Another thought: if I could understand God, I would be His equal. I do not need a God who is equal to me, I need One who is so much greater He is able to control my future, so much wiser He will never make the mistakes I make, and so much more powerful He will save me from myself.

And, I have Him!

One of the hallmarks of a cult is that they mistakenly believe they can explain God. These so-called religions have God "all figured out" and offer pat answers for every question. Imagine how small and impotent God would have to be for humans to figure Him out! The greatest scientific minds cannot understand why only "left-handed" amino acids exist in living cells [more on that a little later], yet some people believe that Almighty God can be understood and explained. That is foolishness!

A Universal Appreciation of God

How are we to grow in appreciation of God when it is impossible to understand Him? Simple—consider His works! Scripture says to gaze at the heavens and you will then appreciate the Heavenly Father!

> *The heavens are telling of the glory of God; and their expanse is declaring the work of His hands. [Psalm 19:1]*

All of God's creation testifies about His existence and magnificence to anyone who will listen. I think this is especially evident when you consider the universe.

I love to go to the High Sierras...especially now that I am a Christian. There is something about the night sky that proclaims the glory of God to me...all those incredible stars, so numerous they just blur together [that is why they call it "the Milky Way"!].

God created these wonders, then created something in us that recognizes them as His handiwork. Paul explained it beautifully to the Romans:

> *That which is known about God is evident within them; for God made it evident to them. For since the creation of the world His invisible attributes, His eternal power and divine nature, have been clearly seen. [Romans 1:19-20]*

Look at a baby, an ocean or the solar system...you see absolute proof that God exists. Some scientists try to deny God by discrediting creation, but they are betraying their own God-given conscience with prideful conjecture.

Spanning the Heavens

Who has measured the waters in the hollow of His hand, and marked off the heavens by the span, and calculated the dust of the earth by the measure, and weighed the mountains in a balance, and the hills in a pair of scales?
[Isaiah 40:12]

In Isaiah's time, a span was the distance between the tips of the thumb and the little finger. The prophet says that is what God used to measure our earth and sky.

I measured my span and it is eight and three-eighths inches–about the width of a standard sheet of copy paper. God's span is infinitely immense! Imagine...in the palm of one hand He can hold all the water in the world—water covers two thirds of the earth's surface and is six miles deep in some places! The universe is so wide that it is not measured in miles but by the length of time it takes for light to travel from one end to the other, yet God measured it with the span of His hand.

How big is that? Scientists say the universe is about ten billion light years across and expanding.

A light year is the distance light is able to travel in one year—almost 6 trillion miles! That translates to six hundred and seventy million [670,000,000] miles per hour...one hundred eighty six thousand, two hundred eighty two [186,282] miles per second!

Allow me to try to put some perspective on that speed:

- The circumference of the earth at the equator is twenty four thousand, nine hundred two [24,902] miles. It takes light one seventh of a second to travel that distance.

- The moon is approximately two hundred thirty thousand [230,000] miles from earth. A jet traveling from the earth to the moon at five hundred miles per hour would take almost 20 days to make the trip...it takes light 1.3 seconds.

- The sun is ninety three million [93,000,000] miles from earth. A jet flying five hundred miles per hour would take twenty-one years to go the distance...it takes light only eight minutes!

- Proxima Centauri, the star nearest the earth, is 4.3 light years away. For you to see that starlight on earth it has to travel 670,000,000 miles per hour for more than 4 years. A jet flying at 500 miles per hour would take fifty-one trillion [51,000,000,000,000] hours to make the same trip [5,771,535.7 years]!

You and I cannot imagine that amount of time...and this is merely the nearest star! Most stars in our solar system are between one hundred and one thousand light years from earth; some stars in our galaxy are 4,000 light years away. The light you see from those stars tonight began traveling at about the time Moses crossed the Red Sea.

It takes light ten billion years to travel from one end of the universe to the other, yet God created it all in seven days...and it is only as wide as His hand! I cannot help but wonder what other marvelous things might be out there that God created in eternity past.

Amazing Methods and Wondrous Results

God's creative method is as amazing as His creative genius.

By the word of the LORD the heavens were made, and by the breath of His mouth all their host. He gathers the waters of the sea together as a heap; He lays up the deeps in storehouses. Let all the earth fear the LORD; let all the inhabitants of the world stand in awe of Him. For He spoke, and it was done; He commanded, and it stood fast.
[Psalm 33:6-9]

God simply spoke a word and everything in the universe came into existence. He breathed and the hosts of heaven came alive. He breathed again and a heap of dust became a man.

Then the LORD God formed man of dust from the ground, and breathed into his nostrils the breath of life; and man became a living being. [Genesis 2:7]

What a Marvelous Event!

The human heart beats more than 100,000 times each day...three billion times in the average lifespan of 75 years. It pumps two thousand gallons of blood in a 24-hour period - enough to fill a swimming pool in 2 or 3 days. <u>The vessels that transport blood stretch 60,000 miles if placed end-to-end...that is enough to circle the earth twice</u>! If you practice healthy living, this incredible pump will require no maintenance or repair. No piece of equipment on earth can equal the human heart in performance and efficiency, yet it is essentially dust and the breath of God!

Consider the human foot! It is made up of 26 bones, collectively able to sustain one thousand tons of cumulative force during a soccer game. Engineers have never designed anything as complicated, intricate and durable as the foot [and they never will!].

Look at the workings of the eye. Light enters through the cornea and passes to the iris, which constricts to control the amount of light entering the pupil. Just past the pupil the lens bends the light and focuses it into a narrow beam received by the retina. The retina consists of ten layers of cells that translate the light beam into color, depth and definition. Look up for a moment from this page and consider the things around you in those terms. Amazing, isn't it?

God's Glory Revealed in DNA vs. Darwin

DNA is unsurpassed in its ability to declare the wonder and glory of God. There are roughly seventy five trillion cells in your body, and nearly all contain a small sack called a nucleus, considered the cell's brain. Inside are long, twisted strands of DNA which carry the written instructions a cell needs to function. DNA does not actually do the work, it produces the workers... proteins.

Proteins are made up of chemical compounds called amino acids which have characteristics scientists refer to as "right-handed" and "left-handed." In general, about half of all amino acids are right-handed and the other half are left-handed...with one wonderful exception: DNA!

Every form of life on earth contains only left-handed amino acids. Scientists cannot explain why, but they know that if even one right-handed amino acid is present in a living cell, the cell dies.

This poses a nasty problem for evolutionists because it destroys their theory that life is the result of elements randomly coming together. There are millions of amino acids in a single living cell. It is not possible that only left-handed ones grouped together to create life by sheer chance.

A relatively new finding about DNA has revealed something Charles Darwin himself said would disprove evolution. Darwin admitted his theory would completely fall apart if a complex organ existed that could not possibly have formed by a process of many small, successive changes.

Scientists call this "irreducible complexity." Simply stated, it refers to something that is complex [made up of more than one part] which cannot be reduced to a simpler form and still work.

DNA is irreducibly complex!

It cannot form without protein, and protein cannot form without DNA. It is impossible that either one existed without the other, then at some point evolved until life was formed. [Sorry, Charlie!]

Why are DNA and protein interdependent? Why do only left-handed amino acids exists in living cells? Essentially, it is God saying, "Hello, I'm here!"

The Power of His Word

God's Word is what created the universe and is what keeps everything intact.

57

And He is the radiance of His glory and the exact representation of His nature, and upholds all things by the word of His power. [Hebrews 1:3]

And it will remain so until He speaks something new.

But by His word the present heavens and earth are being reserved for fire, kept for the day of judgment and destruction of ungodly men. But do not let this one fact escape your notice, beloved, that with the Lord one day is like a thousand years, and a thousand years like one day. The Lord is not slow about His promise, as some count slowness, but is patient toward you, not wishing for any to perish, but for all to come to repentance.

But the day of the Lord will come like a thief, in which the heavens will pass away with a roar and the elements will be destroyed with intense heat, and the earth and its works will be burned up. Since all these things are to be destroyed in this way, what sort of people ought you to be in holy conduct and godliness, looking for and hastening the coming of the day of God, because of which the heavens will be destroyed by burning, and the elements will melt with intense heat! But according to His promise we are looking for new heavens and a new earth, in which righteousness dwells. [2 Peter 3:7-13]

God is going to speak into existence a new heaven and a new earth! I believe that means all our normal concepts are off, and things will be completely different from what we know and can imagine.

The writer of Hebrews and Peter had no idea protons, electrons and neutrons existed when they wrote these words. Isn't that amazing? Man did not prove the existence of the atom until centuries later! But through the anointing of the Holy Spirit these men were given understanding that God holds the universe together with a word!

For He spoke, and it was done; He commanded, and it stood fast. [Psalm 33:9]

The Eternal I AM

According to Exodus 3, Moses was standing before a burning bush when God essentially said,

Moses, you are the man I'm looking for! Go to Egypt. I will use you to deliver My people out of slavery.

When God speaks from a burning bush, you do what He says! You would be crazy to refuse! Understandably, Moses was still a little uneasy. He originally left Egypt because he was wanted for murder, so it was understandable that he was not anxious to return!

Moses agreed to do as God instructed but asked,

If I don't tell them who is sending me, they will not listen, so who should I say I represent?

"I am who I am," God replied. "Tell them 'I AM' sent me."

For years I thought God's answer was weird. Was He saying: "I AM God. I AM the Lord. I AM the God Most High."

I am certain Moses walked away from that conversation, scratching his head, exclaiming, "I'm going to tell them 'I AM' sent me?" Moses was an educated man, so God may have been testing his faith. Or perhaps God knew there was no description He could give Moses that the Hebrew slaves would understand. They did not have the Bible as we do today, and did not know that God is:

Elohim, the Creator
El-Elyon, God Most High
El-Roi, the God Who Sees All
El-Shaddai, God All Sufficient
Adonai, the Self-Existent One
Jehovah-Jireh, the Lord Who Provides
Jehovah-Rophe, the Lord who heals
Jehovah-Saboath, the Lord of Hosts

God spoke the only thing they could understand, "Moses, just tell them that I AM. I AM yesterday, I AM now and I AM the future." God is eternal so He always IS. I think His message to Moses was: "You have a beginning and an end—but I AM."

God's eternal nature is another of His traits we simply cannot fathom.

Our Omnipresent, Omniscient God

God is eternal, omniscient [knows and understands all things at all times] and omnipresent [in all places at all times].

Think about that for a moment! God knows who every person is, where they are, what they are doing, what each is feeling, thinking and saying...plus He knows all the effects these things will have.[Psalm 139:2, 4; Psalm 44:21; Jeremiah 17:10] There are six billion people on this planet and He has complete awareness, understanding and insight about each one...every moment, every day. It is beyond comprehension!

Where can I go from Your Spirit? Or where can I flee from Your presence? If I ascend to heaven, You are there; if I make my bed in Sheol, behold, You are there. If I take the wings of the dawn, if I dwell in the remotest part of the sea, even there Your hand will lead me, and Your right hand will lay hold of me. [Psalm 139:7]

David understood the omnipresence of God; he knew he could hide nothing.

Sometimes I think about that and feel ashamed because there are occasions when I allow myself to have ungodly, dishonoring thoughts. I cannot hide those from God and show Him only my righteous thoughts.

Christians who believe they can do things in secret are wrong. God sees every detail! [Men, when you switch on the computer and click on to a pornographic site, God is right there with you, asking, "What are you doing, My son?"]

Praise God that He forgives us and does not leave us hopelessly at the mercy of our minds! He has given us the ability to take every thought captive to the obedience of Christ. [2 Corinthians 10:5].

The way I see it, we may not be able to help which thoughts come into our minds, but we certainly can determine which ones stay there! Jesus gives us power to cast down any thoughts that dishonor God, but we must choose to reject them.

The God of the Future

Because God is not limited by time and space, He is able to be with us in the present having already visited the future! He knows what will happen to you tomorrow...next week...next year...in one thousand years! That is comforting to me. Since God knows my future, He is preparing my way, ready to handle anything that comes.

The LORD your God is the One who goes ahead of you; He will be with you. He will not fail you nor forsake you.
[Deuteronomy 31:8]

I share this scripture with people in the hospital who are about to have surgery. It is comforting to know God has already been in the operating room, gone through the surgery, and knows the outcome. Nothing that happens will catch Him off guard; they can trust that He is in control. That truth imparts great peace—even in the face of death.

The Omnipotent God

Another of God's incomprehensible qualities is omnipotence. He is all-powerful all the time! When the Angel Gabriel visited the Virgin Mary and told her she was going to have a child, she essentially replied, "There is one small problem. I have never been with a man."

I can just imagine a smiling Gabriel replying, "Please, Mary! This is not a problem for God. He is more powerful than your small, humble mind can understand. I have seen God do some amazing things and believe me, putting a baby in your womb is no problem. He can do that in His spare time. He speaks the word, girl, and you are pregnant!"

When you choose to appreciate God's power it gives greater meaning to Philippians 4:13:

I can do all things through Christ who strengthens me.
[NKJV]

With the unlimited power of God available to you through Jesus, what can possibly defeat you? Only unbelief! No matter what happens in your life, God has gone before you, is not caught unprepared and is powerful enough to lead you through it. He is able to move any mountain in any situation unless you choose to believe that He cannot or will not. As my brother, Mark, so eloquently says it, "God responds to your faith, not to your needs."

The Power to Answer Prayers...Positively!

Being a pastor, I have had many opportunities to see God miraculously lead, comfort, strengthen, heal, deliver, provide, change lives, fulfill His promises and answer prayer. People are not always pleased with God's answer, but His ways are superior.

In my book, *Prayer Can Change Your World*, I explain that God always answers "yes" to a Christian's prayer. He says it in one of four ways:

"Yes!"
"Yes, in a little while."
"Yes, here's the solution."
"Yes, but not the way you think...it will be *better!*"

Sometimes Christians wrongly think God's answer is "no" because what they envision when making a request is different from what God actually delivers. I have come to believe that God does not say "no" to prayers.

For years I asked God to give me a wife. There were times I thought He must be saying "no" because I was getting older and still was not married. What He was really saying was, "Yes, in a little while." He eventually gave me a wonderful wife who is better than I imagined and more than I deserve. Mary is one of the kindest, most gentle people I have ever been privileged to know.

God gave me the desire of my heart at a time when I could receive and appreciate the gift of His precious daughter. I still had plenty of growing to do, but I had matured enough to know the value of humility. As I have been willing to be humble before God and Mary, He has lifted me up and blessed me! I am thankful that He said, "Yes, but not now," instead of "yes" when I first began asking for a wife.

God has answered "yes" to every request I have made. For years I prayed fervently that He would anoint my preaching and use me to inspire people to follow Him. I am continually amazed and thankful when I see God encouraging, teaching and loving His people through me.

I used to have an obvious stutter and asked God to deliver me. Today I regularly preach three weekend services without any noticeable impediment.

Some of my financial requests that God has answered "yes" to have been so magnificent they are illogical! In 2001, I realized my mortgage would be paid off within two years. I thought, "How is this possible? By all accounts I should not have been approved for this loan, much less be able to pay it off in 15 years."

When I bought that house I was earning $1200 per month. The representative at the mortgage company said I was wasting my time applying for a home loan because I could not afford one.

I explained that my dad would co-sign the loan for me and that his credit was extremely good. The answer surprised me— my problem was not in receiving a loan, it was in securing mortgage insurance! My income was so small that no company would insure me. According to their figures I would not have enough money left for food and expenses...banking on me would be inviting a sure default!

I offered to rent out rooms to make up the difference, but was told the money would not qualify as income. I truly believed God wanted me to have that house so I asked the mortgage company to wait a couple of days before declining my application.

While I prayed, God worked.

Within two days the mortgage company representative called with a miraculous story! He had explained my situation to a woman in New Jersey who represented a mortgage insurance company. She said, "I don't know why I'm doing this but I'll give him mortgage insurance." The man could not believe it! I not only believed it...I expected it!

As I am writing this chapter another "yes" is being worked out—I am fulfilling my lifelong desire to build my own home!

A Testimony of My Life *and* My God

My favorite scripture is Romans 10:11:

Whoever believes in Him will never be disappointed.

That is the testimony of my life! Every time I have chosen to trust God, He has surpassed my hopes. I am not perfect—I have failed many times, but I have also tried very hard to obey and fear the Lord.

The miracles God has worked on my behalf are not because I am exceptional. I do not have a special anointing on my life because I am a pastor. The Bible says that God does not show partiality [Deuteronomy 10:17; 2 Chronicles 19:7; Acts 19:34-35; Romans 2:11]. I believe when God called me into ministry He simply looked out at a crowd of people and said, "I need a pastor. You there, Dave Hoffman...you will do."

The blessings I have received are not the result of knowing special secrets, using formulas or being an exceptional person...they are simply because I have made the decision to fear the Lord.

Who Would *NOT* Appreciate God?

Who could possibly see God's magnificent work and *not* appreciate Him? Sadly, there are many!

People who refuse to believe He exists top the list. Atheists and agnostics cannot fully appreciate the miracles of creation without accepting the Creator of miracles. They witness His work but attribute it to ridiculous processes that never occurred. They miss its highest purpose - to express God's great love for mankind!

Some believers fail to appreciate God because they do not fear Him. The reason is clear—He is not a priority. Things of the world rank higher than developing an intimate relationship with God. There is time for television but not Bible reading...they take a phone everywhere but rarely call on God in prayer...they listen to the world's recommendation for finding happiness but do not make time to hear God's still, small voice.

However, some choose to fear God and grow in appreciation of Him. They try to live according to His Word and make serving Him a priority. As a result the blessings abound! They enjoy wonderful rewards in this life—the greatest of which are friendship and intimacy with the Creator of the Universe.

In eternity, even more blessings await those who fear the Lord!

CHAPTER FOUR

Learning to Fear the Lord

Did you know that there are twice as many scriptures in the Bible about fearing the Lord as there are about the love of God? That used to perplex me, but I believe I have come to understand the reason why. As we've previously seen, the fear of the Lord involves an understanding that there are consequences for disobedience and blessing for obedience. Both of these principles are rooted in God's love for us.

As you obey God, you receive blessings. Over time a deep affection toward God develops within you because you begin to understand the depth of His love for you. You realize He did not have to give you His Word, His blessings, or die for you...He *chose* to because He loves you! As your relationship with Him matures, you recognize the deep love that even drives His discipline. I am convinced that if you want to understand the love of God you must first fear Him.

Leading in the Fear of the Lord

One of the strongest messages woven throughout the Old Testament is the value of fearing the Lord...it was an important theological concept for a godly Israelite. There are countless examples of the abundant blessings that occur when God's people obey Him, and unfortunately, countless examples of catastrophes and crises when they do not.

King Jehoshaphat was one ruler over Judah who feared God and understood His love. Jehoshaphat tried very hard to bring God's law back into the kingdom, in part by appointing court judges and charging them to do their job using godly standards.

He said to the judges, "Consider what you are doing, for you do not judge for man but for the LORD who is with you when you render judgment. Now then let the fear of the LORD be upon you; be very careful what you do, for the LORD our God will have no part in unrighteousness or partiality or the taking of a bribe. [2 Chronicles 19:6-7]

Knowing that God is omnipresent should impact your actions! That was Jehoshaphat's message. He essentially told his judges, "Remember, when you make a judgment, God is right there. Keep that thought in mind as you execute your duty. Think about His principles in the law, what He would want you to do."

Jehoshaphat knew the history of Judah's kings and had seen what happened when they disobeyed God. He was determined that during his reign the fear of God would return to the kingdom of Judah, and it would start at the top. He knew the fear of God was essential to receiving God's blessing.

What was true for King Jehoshaphat is true for you.

The Bible says God does not change—He is the same yesterday, today and forever [Hebrews 13:8]. If you want blessing, knowledge, wisdom, and an abundant life you must respond as Jehoshaphat did...you must fear and obey God.

Many American Christians fail to live the abundant life God has promised because they have what some call "fire insurance" —they are saved and heaven-bound, but do not fear God. People with "fire insurance" rarely overcome problems and hardships – their lives are not victorious because they regularly disobey God's Word and invite consequences.

Learning to Fear the Lord

Fear of the Lord *must* be learned...it does not come naturally. Jeremiah 17:9 says the heart is more deceitful than all else and is desperately sick. I have seen the reality of that truth in my own life. When left to myself, 7 out of 10 times I make wrong decisions. I do not think as God thinks, so I need His leading to act in wisdom. Sensitivity to His direction is the result of fearing Him and coming to know Him.

There are basically four ways we learn how to fear the Lord:

1. Choose to be obedient
2. Reject the fear of man
3. Give up idols
4. Study God's Word

Choose To Be Obedient

Proverbs 1:29-30 essentially says that when we obey God we fear Him. Fearing the Lord is simply making the choice to be obedient. When we do, God gives us the ability to understand His principles as we read His Word. Those principles impart wisdom on how to live...the result is the abundant life Jesus came to provide.

> *I came that they may have life, and have it abundantly.*
> *[John 10:10]*

Faith is required to obey God. In faith you must believe God knows what is best for you and then obey Him. You may not understand why, and will often be required to act contrary to what you think and feel. If you have experienced this, you know that there are times when your emotions are screaming at you to do one thing and the Word of God and His Spirit are guiding you in a different direction. It is as if God is saying, "Please, do not listen to your heart! Go My way and be blessed."

> *Come, you children, listen to me; I will teach you the fear of the LORD. Who is the man who desires life, and loves length of days that he may see good? Keep your tongue from evil, and your lips from speaking deceit. Depart from evil, and do good; seek peace, and pursue it.*
> *[Psalm 34:11-14]*

David is essentially saying that if you want to have a long, abundant life...the kind of life God planned for you...choose to fear Him, depart from evil, be honest and obey His Word.

One of my favorite scriptures is Isaiah 8:13-14:

It is the LORD of hosts whom you should regard as holy. And He shall be your fear, and He shall be your dread. Then He shall become a sanctuary.

I love this verse because it says that when Christians choose to fear God He becomes their sanctuary. In the Old Testament a sanctuary was the place where the presence of God resided. When you choose to obey God, He becomes *your* sanctuary. You are able to sense His presence in every situation because He is there to help you. He will go ahead of you and guide you. He has already been to your future and has provided specifically for each situation. When a problem materializes, God has been there and is ready to guide you through it—*despite what you think or feel!* The only requirement to navigate through life's difficulties is that you ask His direction.

Sanctuary is a refuge. When you choose to be obedient you can live above your problems. Jesus said,

In the world you have tribulation, but take courage; I have overcome the world. [John 16:33]

Hardships will come, but you are able to enjoy victory over them and live in the peace that passes all understanding.

The opposite is also true. If you choose *not* to fear God, you will not live victoriously, you will not overcome hardships, and you certainly will not have peace.

So many Christians suffer needlessly, living with worry, depression and anxiety; they do not overcome problems...their problems overcome them. They know God, but do not live in His provision for their needs because they have areas in their lives where they do not fear Him. I have lived that way, and it is no way to live!

The abundant life God has prepared for you is available when you choose to obey His Word despite your feelings, thinking and understanding.

Reject the Fear of Man

Every person has experienced the fear of man, commonly called *peer pressure*. It often comes when a family member, friend, neighbor, fellow student, coworker or supervisor puts pressure on you to do something contrary to God's Word. When being liked and accepted becomes more important than pleasing God, and you say or do something that compromises or contradicts what you believe, you've succumbed to peer pressure.

At times I have been more concerned about what other people thought about me than what God thought. Worse yet, I have placed the opinions of complete strangers above God!

Everyone experiences peer pressure, here are some examples:

"Come on! We all want you to be there. You don't want to be the only person who doesn't go, do you?"

"Stop the holy-roller stuff and live a little! You will *not* go to hell if you do this!"

"How do you *know* you don't like it? You've never tried it! You might be missing out on something great."

"Come on! What do you mean you don't have sex with your boyfriend? It's natural to have sex!"

"You are not a virgin are you? What is wrong with you...don't you like girls?"

"Look, this is the way we do business. If you're going to work here, you have to play by our rules."

"Christianity is okay on Sunday morning, but this is the *real* world. If you don't compromise a little, you lose money."

The pressure can be immense—but fearing God means caring more about Him than others. Sometimes it requires you to take a stand for righteousness that costs you dearly.

This is nothing new. The Apostle Peter faced fierce peer pressure when he went before the Sanhedrin—the religious leaders of his day. As children, Peter and the other apostles probably were taught that the Sanhedrin men were the most holy in all of Israel. They understood God's Word better than most Jews, were God's anointed, and had the spiritual authority in Judaism. God was with them and they were to be obeyed.

The Sanhedrin told Peter to stop preaching in the name of Jesus, but he refused:

> *When they had brought them, they stood them before the Council. The high priest questioned them, saying, 'We gave you strict orders not to continue teaching in this name, and yet, you have filled Jerusalem with your teaching, and intend to bring this man's blood upon us, but Peter and the apostles answered, 'We must obey God, rather than men.' [Acts 5:27-29]*

Here Peter and the Apostles are being confronted by the highest authority in all Israel and they simply answered, "We must obey God rather than men."

That is rejecting the fear of man no matter what anybody tells you—the President of the United States, the Supreme Court, even an angel! If an angel appeared to you and told you to do something contrary to the Word of God, reject it! That angel is not from God [Galatians 1:8].

Rejecting the fear of man is worth whatever price you pay. I have known a number of people who lost jobs because they feared God more than man...God gave them better jobs. Sometimes He chooses to provide in miraculous ways. There is no formula for how God will respond, but you can be certain of this—when you obey God you place yourself in God's protection and invite His provision and blessing.

Rejecting the fear of man might mean you lose a relationship. Do you really want to be yoked together with someone who does not want you to obey the Word of God? If you are unmarried and in a relationship with a friend or potential spouse who is trying to influence you to live contrary to God's Word, the best thing you can do is run the other way! Get out of that relationship...please! If you obey God instead, you will never be sorry! God has wonderful promises for those who sacrifice relationships to follow Him.

> *And He said to them, 'Truly I say to you, there is no one who has left house or wife or brothers or parents or children, for the sake of the kingdom of God, who will not receive many times as much at this time and in the age to come, eternal life.' [Luke 18:29-30]*

Understand this—if you are married to an unbeliever, I am not saying you should divorce simply because they are trying to pull you away from God. When you married you made a covenant before God and He expects you to honor that covenant. The Bible is very clear about divorce for a believer—being married to an unbeliever is not grounds for divorce [1 Corinthians 7].

Give Up Idols

When God issued the Ten Commandments to the Israelites, His highest priority was that they have no idols.

> *Then God spoke all these words, saying, 'I am the LORD your God, who brought you out of the land of Egypt, out of the house of slavery. You shall have no other gods before Me. You shall not make for yourself an idol, or any likeness of what is in heaven above or on the earth beneath or in the water under the earth. You shall not worship them or serve them; for I, the LORD your God, am a jealous God, visiting the iniquity of the fathers on the children, on the third and the fourth generations of those who hate Me, but showing loving kindness to thousands, to those who love Me and keep My commandments.' [Exodus 20:1-6]*

It is unlikely that you have a five-foot statue in your home that you bow to in worship every day, but you may have idols. Anything we place higher than God is an idol. For some, idols are money, cars, a boat, or a big house. For others it is their job, prestige, or power. Relationships, acceptance, or a lifelong dream may also be idols. Even fear of man can be an idol for some people.

You can identify idols by answering this simple question:

"What keeps me from obeying God and doing what He wants me to do?"

Your answer reveals the idols in your life.

I am saddened when someone tells me they cannot give up something because it means too much to them. What they are really saying is that they are going to worship that thing or person instead of God.

Sometimes a person's actions speak louder about their idols than anything they say. People who refuse to forgive often make an idol of *self*. It has many faces...self-pity, self-centeredness, self-importance, self-righteousness, and so on. When someone refuses to forgive, they are refusing to obey God's command to forgive and are bowing to the idol of self.

As a pastor I have seen people make idols of just about everything...relationships, money, fishing, racing, hobbies, pursuit of fun, and retreat. Some people make an idol of television. There is nothing wrong with watching television, but when it *controls* a person's time to the detriment of their relationships with God and family—*it is an idol!* None of these things are bad in themselves— it is when they are given importance above God that they become idols.

I know a man in his mid-thirties who was promoted to the fifth highest position in a national corporation. He moved his family to a mid-western town to take a job earning more money than he had ever imagined. He bought a huge house, several cars, worked in a big office, had a prestigious career, and respect in his field. By the world's standards he had it all. One morning his wife told him she did not love him and left. I will never forget his response! He said, "I realized that I didn't have anything! I had money, possessions, and prestige but in reality I didn't have anything."

He had made an idol of his career and, like any false god, it betrayed him—it cost him his family! He resigned his job, took another and made the Lord and his family his first priority. Some people thought he was crazy, but he learned an important lesson—only God is able to make life complete. He determined he would obey God, even if his marriage never reconciled. He told me, "I've been to the top and it isn't so good."

Friend, if you want to learn how to fear God you must lay every idol at the foot of the cross. In time the Lord may give some things back to you when He knows there is no danger. Today if you want to fear God you must lay down all those things that keep you from obeying God. A friend of mine, Marc Dupont, has a prophetic ministry. He gave up mountain climbing when it became an idol to him. He thought about it day and night. It was so important to him that it interfered with his relationship with the Lord. He knew that in order to obey God he must stop...so he did. Years later he started mountain climbing again, but it was no longer an idol he worshipped – it was something fun to do occasionally.

If you want to learn how to fear God you must be willing to give up anything that is an idol in your life.

Study the Word of God

Proverbs 2:1-5 says:

My son, if you will receive my words, and treasure my commandments within you, make your ear attentive to wisdom, incline your heart to understanding; for if you cry for discernment, lift your voice for understanding; if you seek her as silver, and search for her as for hidden treasures; then you will discern the fear of the LORD, and discover the knowledge of God.

Solomon is essentially saying that if you learn about and treasure God's principles and commands...if you pray for knowledge and understanding...God will give you the wisdom to apply those principles in your life.

Fearing the Lord begins with learning the Word of God. If you are faced with something and do not know what scripture says about it, ask someone to show you. When you discover what the Word says—do it!

> *Remember the day you stood before the LORD your God at Horeb, when the LORD said to me, 'Assemble the people to Me, that I may let them hear My words so they may learn to fear Me all the days they live on the earth, and that they may teach their children.' [Deuteronomy 4:10]*

Moses was reminding the Israelites how important it was that they remember and obey God's Word. He knew that would impart the fear of the Lord, which invokes God's protection, provision, and blessing!

When you read the Word of God you learn His principles. As you obey them you reap the benefits and your commitment to God grows. And remember, we teach these principles to our children primarily through the way we live. My children know that before I make decisions I seek God's counsel through His Word.

God's Inspired Word or Antiquated History?

I have shared with you how God saved my life from an overdose of drugs. After I had been walking with God for a time, I realized I was at a crossroad and needed to decide one very important thing—whether I believed the Bible was really God's Word! In college I read a great deal and formed some philosophies that shaped many of my lifestyle choices. Some of those choices were contrary to God's Word. I believed He existed, but was not so certain He actually inspired the writings of the Bible.

"Even if the Bible is inspired," I questioned, "is it really relevant today? When the apostles wrote these things they had cultural biases and lacked the knowledge we have today. I need to filter the Bible through this understanding when I read it."

Interestingly, when I first went to a liberal seminary this was the basic philosophy of most of the professors and students. I finally came to this conclusion: "If God's Word is true, then it should manifest itself in the lives of people who obey it. Their lives should be diametrically opposed to the lives of Christians who disobey and compromise."

I was essentially raised in church. My father was a pastor; I knew some families who had been in his church for 25 years. I began looking over names in the church directory. Within fifteen minutes I was convinced that the Bible is the Word of God! Those families who were committed to obeying God were blessed. Their marriages were blessed. If their children rebelled, it was short-lived and they usually returned to God.

I looked at other families who were always in church on Sunday, but did not include God or His Word in the rest of their week. Their lives showed it!

Four hundred years before Israel had its first King, Moses offered some valuable advice:

> *Now it shall come about when [the king] sits on the throne of his kingdom, he shall write for himself a copy of this law on a scroll in the presence of the Levitical priests. It shall be with him, and he shall read it all the days of his life, that he may learn to fear the LORD his God, by carefully observing all the words of this law and these statutes, that his heart may not be lifted up above his countrymen and that he may not turn aside from the commandment, to the right or the left, so that he and his sons may continue long in his kingdom in the midst of Israel. [Deuteronomy 17:18-20]*

Moses was essentially saying, "You are going to have a king, and when you do, make certain he writes out every word of God's law. Have him write it so that it will be branded on his mind and have a priest confirm that that which he writes is correct."

Israel's king needed to memorize God's Word because his actions would impact the entire nation. If he did not make reading God's Word a priority, he might easily forget it, fall into pride and come to believe that he knew better than God how to lead God's people.

Friend, the same is true for you. You need to read God's Word regularly. Allow Him to write it on your heart so that you will fear and obey Him.

Revival's One Requirement...YOU!

I am hungry for revival in my church, Foothills Christian Fellowship, and throughout San Diego County, where my church is located. I want people to come to church on Sunday morning and encounter the presence of God in such power that the unsaved are converted, the back-slidden convicted, the depressed are revived, people are healed, delivered, and forgiven. I want our worship to draw the Spirit of God in a powerful way.

If revival comes to Foothills it will be wonderful, but I am hoping it comes to most area churches. There are numerous examples in America where the power of God has moved in one church, but not transformed the community. If the Spirit of God were to move in many churches at the same time it would bring change! Revival would be the topic of conversation at police stations, in bars and on school campuses.

That is what I am praying will happen!

My brother Mark and I pray that God will rend the heavens and shower His power over our entire community. It makes no difference if it starts with us or not, we just want to be part of what God is doing!

How does revival of that magnitude happen? You have probably heard the saying, "If you want revival, draw a circle and step into it." That is true. Revival happens one person at a time. First and foremost you must fear God...you must choose to obey Him, reject the fear of man, give up every idol in your life, and study the Word of God. It will completely change your life...the way you think and communicate with people; it will change your marriage and how you deal with your children; it will impact the way you do business and see your neighbors. These four steps that lead to one learning how to fear the Lord will most certainly change your life. If a few thousand people in a community began to fear the Lord, the community certainly would be affected.

Revival begins with you and me. Often, Christians hope someone else will usher in revival so they can step into the blessing. They want the presence of God, but do not invite it by fearing Him.

God promises to bless those who fear Him. Psalm 128 says:

How blessed is everyone who fears the LORD, who walks in His ways. When you shall eat of the fruit of your hands, you will be happy and it will be well with you. Your wife shall be like a fruitful vine within your house, your children like olive plants around your table. Behold, for thus shall the man be blessed who fears the LORD.
[Psalm 128:1-4]

There are so many wonderful points in this passage! Verse 1 declares that *everyone* who fears the Lord receives God's blessing. Verse 2 promises success in your work and a sense of accomplishment in your life. Some people think verse 3 means you will have children when you marry, but I believe it means something different—when you choose a spouse, use the criteria God would use to choose a spouse for you. Pray about it...make sure he or she fears God. If you do that you will be blessed in marriage.

The second half of the verse addresses the blessings of children. It must be an amazing feeling for a parent whose 16 or 17 year-old son or daughter loves and follows God. Perhaps their child is 21 or 25 and married to a believer who loves God. What a blessing! What could possibly top having your children grow up to serve God?

Verse 4 says anyone who decides to fear the Lord will be blessed.

The four ways we have examined so you can learn to fear the Lord all come down to one thing: choice!

- Will you obey God?
- Will you reject the fear of man?
- Will you demolish idols in your life?
- Will you make the study of His Word part of your daily life?

In the strength of the Holy Spirit you have the power to do all of these things. The choice to learn to fear God is yours!

CHAPTER FIVE

Fearing God with Your Finances

'Bring the whole tithe into the storehouse, so that there may be food in My house, and test Me now in this,' says the LORD of hosts, 'if I will not open for you the windows of heaven, and pour out for you a blessing until it overflows. Then I will rebuke the devourer for you.'

[Malachi 3:10,11]

What a wonderful promise from God! When you fear Him with your finances [when you're obedient], He will shower you with blessings, then protect all He has given to you. What does it mean to fear God with your finances? It begins with having the right perspective about ownership. These four scriptures provide a good foundation for that:

Everything in the heavens and earth is yours, O Lord, and this is your kingdom. We adore you as being in control of everything. Riches and honor come from you alone, and you are the Ruler of all mankind; your hand controls power and might, and it is at your discretion that men are made great and given strength.

[1 Chronicles 29:11-12 Living Bible]

Behold, to the LORD your God belong heaven and the highest heavens, the earth and all that is in it.

[Deuteronomy 10:14]

The earth is the Lord's, and all it contains, The world, and those who dwell in it. [Psalm 24:1]

For the earth is the Lord's and all it contains.

[1 Corinthians 10:26]

and took the stone he had used as a pillow and poured oil on it saying:

This stone, which I have set up as a pillar, will be God's house, and of all that You give me I will surely give a tenth to you. [Genesis 28:22]

Several hundred years later, when God revealed His will to Moses, tithing ceased to be optional—God commanded it from His people.

Thus all the tithe of the land, of the seed of the land or of the fruit of the tree, is the LORD's; it is holy to the LORD.
[Leviticus 27:30]

God called the tithe 'holy to Himself'...it is set apart for Him alone! That was His will for the Israelites then and it is His will for you and me today. God provides one hundred percent of all you have, but He has given you permission to use only ninety percent of it. The tithe is not ours to keep.

Is Tithing Obsolete?

The fact that God expects His people to tithe is irrefutable when you consider all that is written about it in scripture. There are some who claim otherwise, but they misuse scripture to control the use of their money instead of submitting it to God. This is blatant *rebellion*!

The arguments I have heard to support the idea that tithing is no longer required are based on an exegesis that cannot withstand scrutiny using the original Greek and Hebrew texts. Jesus was clear that He was not abolishing the Law, which included the command to tithe [Matthew 5:17].

If you are among those who believe tithing is obsolete I am not questioning your salvation, nor will I like you less. This issue is between you and God. But I guarantee, you will not experience the financial blessing reserved for those who trust and obey God with their finances.

My wife Mary and I tithe faithfully...it is the first thing we do with our income. We have been blessed beyond our ability to comprehend. We have also seen God work countless miracles on our behalf. We love to see God glorified in our finances, but there is another reason I am committed to tithing—I am afraid *not* to tithe! Though I am still learning what it means to fear God with my finances, I have seen enough to know that it is dangerous to be cavalier with God's holy portion. As a pastor, I see people all the time paying a high price for keeping money that is rightfully God's.

God's Perspective on Tithes

God offered His perspective on tithing through the prophet Malachi. Though it is recorded in the Old Testament, Malachi's message is God's instruction to His people and is as relevant today as it was when He first spoke it. If you are a Christian, God's message through Malachi is for you.

A remnant of Jews had returned to Jerusalem from Babylonian captivity. They rebuilt the city and made a covenant with God to obey His Word in every way, but after two generations [about one hundred years] they began compromising many of God's commands. Society experienced serious problems including the loss of prosperity. The people began to call out to the God they had ignored and disobeyed, essentially saying, "God, what is wrong? We are the sons and daughters of Abraham! Why are you withholding blessing from us?" God responded through Malachi, explaining that they had compromised many things, including tithes.

'From the days of your fathers you have turned aside from My statutes and have not kept them. Return to Me, and I will return to you,' says the LORD of hosts. 'But you say, "How shall we return?" Will a man rob God? Yet you are robbing Me! But you say, "How have we robbed You?" In tithes and offerings. You are cursed with a curse, for you are robbing Me, the whole nation of you! Bring the whole tithe into the storehouse, so that there may be food in My house, and test Me now in this,' says the LORD of hosts, 'if I

will not open for you the windows of heaven, and pour out for you a blessing until it overflows. Then I will rebuke the devourer for you, so that it will not destroy the fruits of the ground; nor will your vine in the field cast its grapes,' says the LORD of hosts. 'All the nations will call you blessed, for you shall be a delightful land,' says the LORD of hosts. [Malachi 3:7-12]

Just like generations before and since these people entered a covenant with God, followed Him for a time then compromised.

The Lord makes four basic declarations about tithing in this passage from Malachi:

1. If you are not giving tithes and offerings you are **robbing God!**

2. If you are not tithing your finances are **under a curse!**

3. The tithe must be brought into **the storehouse!**

4. **"Test Me!"** Obey God with tithes to test His faithfulness.

Robbing God

God's first declaration appears in verses 7 and 8. By failing to give tithes and offerings the Jews were **robbing God**. If you have ever had something stolen from you, you know that the offense goes beyond material loss—the perpetrator is violating and dishonoring you!

Vehicles have been stolen from me twice! One was outside my church and the other was in my driveway. Both times I asked the police if I could expect to get my vehicles back and was told that in all probability they were in Mexico and gone forever. [San Diego is close to the Mexican border where vehicles are stolen to be sold on the black market.] Instead of resigning myself to statistics I went to the Lord in prayer. Both vehicles were returned to me! I do not think it is coincidence that my property was recovered against insurmountable odds. I had been tithing faithfully for years!

Chances are you would not steal a car or sneak into a neighbor's house to take his stereo, television, or jewelry. Yet some who would never think of stealing from another person regularly rob God by keeping for themselves the portion of income God has called holy and His alone. Their actions violate and dishonor Him.

Under a Curse

God's second declaration is in verse 9 – if you do not tithe your finances are **under a curse**. The curse is not stated but is implied in verse 11:

If you tithe I will rebuke the devourer from you.

Since tithing engages God's protection against the devourer, failure to tithe gives the devourer access to your finances—that is the curse! In the financial arena refusing to tithe is tantamount to rejecting God's protection!

The Hebrew word translated "devourer" in this scripture is *'akal.'* It means, "to eat, devour, BURN UP." It never refers to something good. This is no surprise—the devourer is Satan!

According to 1 Peter 5:8 Satan prowls around like a roaring lion, seeking someone to devour. The Greek word in this scripture that is translated "devour" is *katapino*, "to drink down." This verse literally means that Satan sneaks around looking for someone to swallow up, drink down, devour and destroy.

The only people the devourer has access to are those who have rejected God's protection through disobedience. If you are not tithing, God allows Satan access to your finances and he consumes them!

You see, friend, the tithe is holy whether you give it to God or not and He will never allow you to keep something holy! When you do not give the tithe to God—the rightful Owner—He allows Satan access to it. Unfortunately when Satan taps into your finances he has full access and does not stop at ten percent. He will gobble up all he can! The dishwasher will break, your car will need repairs, or your son will shoot a BB through the window.

Since you will never see it anyway, why not give the holy tithe to God and receive a blessing in return?

Bring Tithes to the Storehouse

God's third declaration is that the tithe must be brought into **the storehouse**. In Malachi's time the storehouse was the Temple in Jerusalem. There were literal storehouses to stock commodities brought in by God's people...things like chickens, goats, and grains. The priest's job was to provide for the people's spiritual needs and to represent them before God. Priests did not grow crops or tend flocks and herds so the tithe was their provision for food and clothing.

Most scholars agree that the modern storehouse is the local church—the place where God's people are spiritually fed. In Christ we are all priests [1 Peter 2:9 and Revelation 1:6] and may eat the spiritual food in God's house. But some are called to fulltime ministry to prepare and serve the spiritual food to the community of believers. God uses the tithe to provide for the needs of those workers and their families. This is why it is important for the tithe to be brought into the storehouse, or local church. When the local church is not "stocked" by the community of believers, the entire community suffers.

The local church is also where believers' resources are pooled to make a Christ-like impact on the community of unbelievers.

Test Me!

My favorite part of God's point through Malachi is the fourth declaration found in verse 10. Essentially God says, "**Test Me** and see if I will not open up the windows of heaven and pour out blessings until they overflow." God actually invites us to test Him! He knows that giving ten percent is not logical to us and He loves to prove Himself in the face of impossible odds.

The mind reasons that if you give ten percent you will have ten percent less for your children, groceries, bills, the house, and recreation. But we are to reject logic when it contradicts God's Word and instead see in the Spirit. God says He will bless those who tithe. Test Him and you will find you live far better on the ninety percent that remains than you would if you refused Him the tithe and kept it all.

One of the most common arguments in logic is, "I cannot tithe because I do not earn enough." In reality, a person who has a small income cannot afford NOT to tithe! God's miracles are needed most when money is tight and tithing is the only way to give God access to your finances so He can prosper you. When you honor God, He is bound by His Word to bless you. When you tithe you are entitled to remind Him of His promise to bless you, claim it in Jesus' name and wait for His miraculous supply.

Over the years I have seen the faithfulness of God time and time again in the lives of people who have obeyed Him with their finances. When people make a commitment to tithe regardless of their circumstances, God always blesses! The opposite is also true. I have seen people refuse to give God access to their income and they live in chronic financial struggle.

Prosperity Verses Blessing

Throughout the 1990's and early into this century America enjoyed the best economy ever and most Americans prospered. Some Christians prospered even though they did not tithe. That was not God directly blessing them, it was the state of the economy. If they had tithed, generally they would have prospered even more, their savings accounts would have expanded and those who were business owners would have experienced greater growth.

Remember Jesus' parable about the sower? Following godly principles produces a harvest...thirty-fold, sixty-fold and one hundred-fold. In relation to your finances this means that if you tithe and strive to be a good steward you will be better off in two, five, or ten years, than if you would not have followed biblical commands concerning your finances. God's Word proclaims it!

The economy rises and falls. When it peaks even the disobedient may prosper. But when you choose to fear God with your finances you will be blessed apart from what is happening with the economy! I believe this is part of the gospel or good news.

Yet consequences await those who disobey...consequences like living in a perpetual state of lack, accumulating credit card debt, or arguing about money with their spouse. God intended for money to be a tool in the hands of His people but it becomes master over those who misuse it. It is a poor, demanding, insatiable master! Perhaps it is no coincidence it is referred to as "cold, hard" cash!

In my church we offer financial training through Crown Ministries. It is an excellent program that teaches godly principles about handling money. It is also an effective remedial tool for those with financial problems. I believe the reason it works so well is because it is entirely scripture-based. Participants must memorize Bible verses about finances and apply them in weekly homework lessons. God's Word is living and active [Hebrews 4:12] and always produces the results He desires [Isaiah 55:11]. The same God who was crucified rose from the dead and said, "Believe in Me and you will have eternal life" says, "I will bless you if you trust Me with your finances."

An Issue of the Heart

There is no question in my mind that Jesus expected His followers to tithe. One third of His parables deal with money. One sixth of the gospel scriptures refer to money or possessions. God placed great emphasis on this subject because a person's heart is tied to what they treasure [Matthew 6:21].

Tithing is really a test of your heart. It poses the question, "What do you really believe about God's faithfulness and His promises?" It is one thing to believe in eternal life and quite another to trust God with ten percent of your money.

Woe to you, scribes and Pharisees, hypocrites! For you tithe mint and dill and cumin, and have neglected the weightier provisions of the law; justice and mercy and faithfulness; but these are the things you should have done without neglecting the others. [Matthew 23:23]

Jesus essentially said, "You guys are so careful to measure out every speck of dill you can shake from a spice bottle to see that God receives exactly ten percent. But you do not love your neighbor nor value honesty and integrity."

The Pharisees were obsessing over minutia and neglecting weightier things like justice, mercy and faithfulness. Jesus did not tell them to abandon tithing. He called them to continue in their tithing but to also practice justice, mercy, and faithfulness.

I believe this is the only time Jesus gave the Pharisees a pat on the back, essentially saying, "Good job! You are on track with tithing, but the rest of your religious life is a mess!"

> *Then the Pharisees went and plotted together how they might trap Him in what He said. And they sent their disciples to Him, along with the Herodians, saying, 'Teacher, we know that You are truthful and teach the way of God in truth, and defer to no one; for You are not partial to any. Tell us then, what do You think? Is it lawful to give a poll-tax to Caesar, or not?' But Jesus perceived their malice, and said, 'Why are you testing Me, you hypocrites? Show Me the coin used for the poll-tax.' And they brought Him a denarius. And He said to them, 'Whose likeness and inscription is this?' They said to Him, 'Caesar's.' Then He said to them, 'Then render to Caesar the things that are Caesar's; and to God the things that are God's.' And hearing this, they were amazed, and leaving Him, they went away. [Matthew 22:15-22]*

What are "the things that are God's"? Your tithe! Jesus was talking about money in this passage! His message today would be something like this, "You must pay the IRS what is theirs and you must give God what He has called holy to Himself."

Jesus Fulfilled the Law!

Jesus made it clear that He did not intend to bring an end to the observance of God's Law...He intended to fulfill it!

Do not think that I came to abolish the Law or the Prophets; I did not come to abolish, but to fulfill.

[Matthew 5:17]

He fulfilled the Law by living His entire life in perfect obedience to it. He then paid the price for sin and that changed the covenant between God and man [Hebrews 8:6-10:18]—God's people were released from certain requirements, like offering atoning sacrifices.

In the Old Testament God's people received forgiveness of sin by making a yearly animal sacrifice, usually a lamb. The priest would kill the animal and God would accept its blood as payment for sin and grant forgiveness. We now have a more complete understanding of the sacrificial system and we know that the blood of Jesus was the ultimate payment for sin, providing forgiveness to all people who accept Him. The law that required the punishment of death for sin was not abolished, it was fulfilled by Jesus. Those who do not accept His payment for sin must pay the penalty themselves!

Dietary restrictions are another example of how Jesus fulfilled the Law. Certain foods were unclean and God's people were never to eat them. Other foods had to be prepared and eaten according to specific guidelines. Failure to observe these restrictions made a person unclean. The New Testament, however, is clear that in Christ all foods have been made clean and are acceptable for God's people to eat [Romans 14:20]. God did not rescind His laws regarding cleanliness—Jesus' blood provided cleansing [Hebrews 9:22].

Circumcision is another requirement of the Law that was fulfilled in Christ. It was the mark of the covenant between God and His people that all males be circumcised. Yet in the New Testament Paul explains that circumcision of the flesh is replaced with circumcision of the heart for those in Christ – which was God's intention all along [Deuteronomy 30:6]. Instead of God's covenant being performed in the flesh by human hands, it is performed in the heart by the Holy Spirit and is symbolized by baptism [Colossians 2:11-12]. Though some people prefer to circumcise newborn males for health reasons, the New Testament is clear that God no longer requires circumcision of the flesh as a sign of covenant relationship with Him.

The New Testament specifically states that God's people are released from circumcision, dietary restrictions, and animal sacrifices because Jesus fulfilled the Law. If tithing was no longer required, the New Testament would certainly detail how Christ had fulfilled that too—but it does not! Therefore we must conclude from Jesus' own words, and the rest of the New Testament, that tithing has not been done away with.

The Heart of the Law

Jesus introduced some new ideas to God's people when He began His ministry. He revealed that God's Law contained much higher standards than people had inferred. Man looks at the outward appearance, but God looks at the heart [1 Samuel 16:7]. Murder and adultery offer good examples of this.

According to Old Testament Law murder was forbidden. Jesus raised the bar when He revealed God's true intent...hate and contempt are essentially murder in a person's heart! The Old Testament forbids the act of adultery but Jesus revealed that the sin is not only in commission of the act—it is in yielding to an adulterous heart. God's people had equated obedience to the Law with a person's actions but Jesus tied it to the desires of the heart.

In both these examples you see that the New Testament model for obedience challenges believers to exceed the minimum interpretation of the Law. The same is true for giving! Jesus makes it clear that tithing is just the beginning.

Give, and it will be given to you. They will pour into your lap a good measure—pressed down, shaken together and running over. For by your standard of measure it will be measured to you in return [Luke 6:38].

Jesus brought new revelation to Old Testament Law—extravagant giving produces abundant blessing. It is the principle of sowing and reaping. When you sow into God's economy you reap a harvest of blessings!

93

With all my heart I want God to bless you financially. Do you believe God is capable of passing the only test He invites you to give Him? Your actions will certainly speak louder than your words. If you are still not convinced that tithing is possible for you, ask God to increase your faith, not your income. He is anxious to prove to you that His economy works!

Pay Yourself

The second requirement of a trustworthy steward is *pay yourself*. You may find this surprising, but it is scriptural. Luke 10:7 says, *"the laborer is worthy of his wages."*

Paying yourself is not setting aside a certain sum each pay period to spend frivolously. It is saving a percentage of your income to provide for your future needs, your children and the Kingdom of God.

The 10-10-80 Plan

The secret to financial success is what some people call the 10-10-80 plan...tithe ten percent, save ten percent and be a good steward with the remaining eighty percent. Utilizing this plan produces prosperity and financial success.

When I first learned that good stewardship included paying myself I did not see how I could implement it on my income. There was almost nothing left after I paid my tithe and bills because our church was new and I made only $750.00 a month. I did not have my own home, a wife, or family so I lived with members of our church.

Over time our church grew, my salary increased, and so did my savings. Financial success comes from simply establishing a godly plan and sticking to it!

When I examine my financial situation today I see an absolute miracle of God. As I write this chapter I am building my dream house on a hill with a breathtaking view. Recently I was standing near the pool we are building and I thought, "How did this happen?" How can I possibly afford to build a house like this when my average salary over the past 15 years is not much over 30,000 a year? It is the result of God blessing my obedience...for fifteen years I tithed ten percent, saved ten percent and tried to be a good steward with the rest.

There were times when I gave in to the temptation to try to get rich quick, but I learned that I am not good at investing money. I invested in gold futures once and turned a few hundred dollars into a few thousand. Instead of quitting while I was ahead I continued to invest. Eventually I lost the few thousand I had earned and then some! I realized it was not a dependable way of providing for my future. I could have saved myself the pain of that lesson if I had heeded the words of Proverbs 21:5,

Steady plodding brings prosperity; hasty speculation brings poverty. [Proverbs 21:5, Living Bible]

Paving the Way for Prosperity

One of my favorite scriptures is Joshua 1:8,

This book of the law shall not depart from your mouth, but you shall meditate on it day and night, so that you may be careful to do according to all that is written in it; for then you will make your way prosperous, and then you will have success. [Joshua 1:8]

When you commit to knowing and obeying the Word of God, you pave the way for prosperity and success. Obey God's principles on marriage and enjoy a good marriage. Apply biblical truths about child rearing and your children will become godly people. They may stray for a season but they will come back to the Lord. When you apply the truth of God's Word to your finances, you tap in to His economy and He will bless you.

Please understand that I am not saying you will be rich. Some preachers will tell you that if you give one thousand dollars you will receive ten thousand and that God wants you to have a Cadillac. I certainly am not making those claims. I do not know if it would be good for you to have a Cadillac or great wealth. But I do know from scripture and my personal experience that if you faithfully tithe, save, and use godly principles in your spending you will be financially better off in five or ten years than if you do not.

Tithing Testimonies

I have shared some examples from my own life about God's faithfulness to those who tithe, now I would like to share some testimonies from people I know who have feared God with their finances.

During a time when our church needed to raise a large amount of money in a short time I called on some of our most faithful givers for help. This letter is the response I received from one woman:

Dear Dave,

When you told me you were calling us to ask us to give to the church's special project, I was actually excited that my husband and I were given a chance to give to God. We still live paycheck to paycheck, but decided to forego our Christmas present to each other [to give to the cause]. Since the day we started tithing ten percent we have seen such miracles in our lives financially. We built our dream house two years ago, something we never thought would happen. Six months after we started to tithe, things just started to fall into place [no one knows except God how we managed to do it]. We couldn't sell our old house so we figured that God wanted us to keep it and somehow that also worked out. Now we have $80,000 equity in a house that we wouldn't have if we would have sold it and done it 'our way.' We had to go to court last year and when our attorney received our financial statements and tax returns she called me and said, "You know it's going to be very difficult to explain how your family makes it on your income with your expenses. What I'm really going to have a hard time explaining is how you can afford to give so much to your church. On paper this looks impossible!" I laughed and laughed because anyone without faith in God would think that it's impossible.

I told the attorney to tell the judge that no matter what money we give, first and foremost it goes to God. My point in all this is that we are so honored to give anything for God's causes. We tell our friends who think they are so broke that the best way to make it financially is just to give to God first. Dave, I have total faith in God but I'm still amazed when He sends little miracles. Just after I wrote out a check [for the church] a client from my business stopped by with an envelope for me. It had [the money to cover the check] along with a thank you note. In my five years of business, no one has ever done that before."

This wonderful lady and husband provided God with the opportunity to work a miracle on their behalf. She supported God's work and He gave her money to buy Christmas gifts.

Another family sent me this letter:

Dear Dave,

We've been Christians for about five years. I've heard quite a few sermons on tithing. Tithing has been a constant sore spot in our marriage. My husband has had much more faith than I have in this area. He always told me that if we gave ten percent to God He would bless us. So, we came up to the altar on a Sunday morning and I confessed to my husband that I needed him to pray that I would learn to trust God in this area. He did and a real peace came over me. We started tithing. We no longer argue over what we're going to give each week. Together, we calculate how much we made for the week and then write a check for ten percent. Just to let you know how faithful the Lord is, within a month of making this commitment, my husband who is self-employed, received a very large job. This particular job took him only two weeks to complete and it paid him half of what he had made for the whole of last year. I don't know why the Lord chose to instantly bless us but all I know is that we will always tithe ten percent no matter what happens.

This woman learned that tithing is not about money, it is about what you really believe in your heart. Tithing reveals who rules your life and how much you trust God as provider. Martin Luther said, "First there is the conversion of the heart, then the purse."

My Heart for Your Finances

I would like to share my heart with you on one point. My purpose for including this chapter on tithing is not for personal gain. If you are a member of our church I am not trying to access your money through tithes—my provider is the Lord. I include it for the same reason I preach it...so that God's people may be blessed. It is my job as a pastor to communicate God's heart to His people. His heart is to bless you financially and He simply cannot do that if you will not fear Him with your finances.

I have prayed over the message in this chapter. I asked the Holy Spirit to inspire, motivate, encourage, or even rebuke you through my words because my desire is for you to receive God's blessing. I want you to experience the financial miracles God performs on behalf of those who honor His economy, trust His ability to provide, and obey His Word.

CHAPTER SIX

Fearing God by Reading His Word

All Scripture is inspired by God and profitable for teaching, for reproof, for correction, for training in righteousness; so that the man of God maybe adequate, equipped for every good work. [2 Timothy 3:16-17]

You have seen that fearing the Lord is essential if you desire to obey Him and enjoy an abundant life. Fearing the Lord enables you to live victoriously, enjoy a good marriage, raise godly children, and have a life marked by the fruits of the Holy Spirit: love, joy, peace, patience, kindness, goodness, faithfulness, gentleness, and self-control.

These blessings are the result of implementing the two fundamental elements of fearing the Lord...understanding that there are consequences for disobedience and blessing for obedience, and growing in appreciation of who God is.

How can you expect to know which actions result in reward and which bring discipline if you do not read the Bible? How can you expect to grow in appreciation of God if you do not grow in your understanding of His character? Only by reading the Bible will you come to really know God and His commands. If you desire to fear the Lord, Bible reading is not optional...it is mandatory!

The Formula for Failure

Unfortunately, many in the church today do not know the Word of God. They may carry a crisp, new study Bible made of fine leather with their name embossed in gold on the front cover. It may be opened every Sunday morning to the passage being preached...perhaps even underlined and highlighted. But all too often the Bible lies closed on a shelf from one Sunday to the next when it is ceremoniously carried back to church again.

Please do not misunderstand me...bringing a Bible to church and using it during services is good but believers need more than a passage or two from a Sunday sermon to live an abundant, victorious life.

Every Christian has the responsibility to live in a way that glorifies God and that comes from being steeped in His Word. The more scripture you read the more you retain. Apply what you retain and your life will change in a way that brings glory to God! Reading scripture conforms your thinking to God's.

Hosea 4:6 defines what I call the formula for failure:

My people are destroyed for lack of knowledge. Because you have rejected knowledge, I will also reject you from being My priest. Since you have forgotten the law of your God, I will also forget your children.

Christians often fail to experience God's blessings because they do not know the Word of God.

Some do not read the Bible because they know God's Word contradicts their choices. Since the Word condemns the sin they accept, they prefer not to read it, perhaps believing this makes life easier for them. Sadly, these people are deceived. Scripture makes it clear that sin is only pleasant for a season and always results in something much worse than the initial difficulty of choosing to stand in righteousness.

For example, someone who is struggling financially may be tempted to relieve the burden by filing falsified tax returns in order to receive a refund. A person who resists the temptation and files truthfully may continue to struggle for a time while paying their tax debt but eventually they will be free from the burden.

On the other hand, one who yields to the temptation and falsifies the tax return may enjoy a season of financial freedom with the ill-gotten gains, but when their sin finds them out...as Numbers 32:23 ensures it will...the burden of fines, penalties and perhaps time in prison will be significantly more difficult than enduring the hardship of paying the initial tax debt on a truthful return.

Some do not read the Word because they do not think it is relevant. The core of that attitude is haughty and tantamount to calling God a liar! He says that all scripture is inspired by Him and has great value [2 Timothy 3:16-17]. He also states that His Word has specific purposes, which will be achieved [Isaiah 55:11]. Claiming that scripture is archaic or irrelevant is essentially discounting God's assertions. That is a very dangerous thing to do!

Others fear that if they read the Bible they will discover something that requires them to make changes in their life. That is the point! The reading of God's Word transforms lives for good! Whatever is given up for the sake of Jesus is well worth the sacrifice. Ultimately there will be a gain that far outweighs the loss.

Disregarding the Word

Some Christians attempt to disregard portions of scripture because it does not fit in with popular philosophy. They are embarrassed by biblical principles that are culturally unpopular, such as intolerance for homosexuality. Intolerance is not politically correct in today's culture. It is considered unreasonable and discriminatory. Yet the Bible clearly states that sin is not to be tolerated and homosexuality is sin. It is important to separate the sin from the sinner. Intolerance for sin should not become intolerance for the one committing the sin.

Other biblical principles that run counter to the ideas of modern culture involve roles of husbands and wives, how children should be parented, and the handling of finances. Some Christians are ashamed to talk about these issues and would rather compromise on God's Word than look bad in the eyes of the world.

There are translations of the Bible that purpose to soften the miracles of Jesus because miracles are not logical. This is simply a poorly veiled attempt to disregard portions of scripture that offend the human mind. When Jesus walked the earth He healed people and performed miracles. Though it offends the minds of those who crave logic, God still heals people and performs miracles today and that is not changed by efforts to water down the Word of God. I am not presenting suppositions—I am testifying to what I have witnessed. Miraculous things have happened in our church! Miraculous events happen every day to thousands of God's people.

When I was in seminary I heard the argument almost daily that Paul's writings contain his cultural bias, which should be discarded for modern application. That is simply not true. God inspired the writing of scripture and every nuance surrounding its writing was deliberate.

There are some ministers who do not preach sections of the Word of God because they fear people will leave the church or that the truth of God's Word is outdated. Without God's Word church becomes nothing more than a form of entertainment. There is nothing wrong with entertainment but it is no substitute for the Word of God.

I am reminded of a story about a seven year old boy who came home from Sunday school and was asked by his mother, "What did you learn today son?" The boy replied, "Oh, it was really good! I learned about Moses leading the Israelites out of Egypt. They came to the Red Sea but they could not get across so Moses called the Israeli Army's Corps of Engineers and they built a pontoon bridge. As the Israelites crossed the bridge the Egyptian Army approached with tanks and heavy artillery. When the ordnance became stuck in the mud Moses knew this was his chance. He called the Israeli Air Force, which bombed the Egyptian Army and wiped them out!" The boy's mother was horrified! "Is that what they told you in Sunday school?" she asked. "Well, not exactly," the boy replied, "but if I told you what they really said you would never believe me!"

Divine Inspiration...Practical Application

Some people think the Bible is unbelievable and therefore it is irrelevant. Nothing could be farther from the truth. God's Word is not unbelievable, it is supernatural...many of Jesus' acts were supernatural. God is supernatural! Neither is the Bible irrelevant. No book in history even comes close to being as relevant to modern life as the Bible.

I am convinced that mankind has not changed much from ancient times. We drive cars instead of riding horse or chariots and enjoy amazing conveniences but I believe that interpersonal problems...family problems...life problems are relatively unchanged! They have been around for thousands of years and the Bible contains answers that are timeless. It is the handbook for human relations...a roadmap for living a blessed life.

The Word of God is the most practical book ever written. It is the instruction manual for every aspect of life. If you want to be successful, learn what the Word of God says will bring success. If you want to enjoy peace, find out what the Bible says provides peace.

The Bible is God's inspired Word. The word "inspired" means "breathed out." What was written is exactly what God intended.

All Scripture is inspired by God and profitable for teaching, for reproof, for correction, for training in righteousness; so that the man of God may be adequate, equipped for every good work.

[2 Timothy 3:16-17]

The Bible is the exact truth God desires to communicate. Those who refuse to believe it or obey it are wrong...that does not change the fact that the Bible is true. Often the root behind a person's rejection of God's Word is his or her refusal to change. Someone adamantly opposed to forgiving another is likely to reject or discredit the biblical command to forgive. Yet in my experience obedience to the Word of God never fails to result in blessing.

The Bible is inspired from cover to cover and that includes the portions that are difficult to read like Leviticus, Numbers and Deuteronomy, where such things as the laws regarding hygiene, sacrifices, the Sabbath and long genealogies are detailed. I confess I struggle through some of those passages. Yet I am reminded that Matthew chapter four describes how Jesus resisted Satan's temptations in the wilderness by quoting scriptures from Deuteronomy three times!

God Has Been There!

One of my favorite verses in the Bible is Deuteronomy 31:8, which says:

The LORD is the One who goes ahead of you; He will be with you. He will not fail you or forsake you. Do not fear or be dismayed.

If you can grasp that, it will change your entire perspective on life. Imagine how you would respond if you really believed that God has already been where you will be in one hour, tomorrow or next month. Will you have a different view of the automobile accident six months from now knowing God has already been through that crisis and has prepared the way for you?

When you really believe Deuteronomy 31:8, nothing will shake you. Instead you will likely say, "Oh well, this is bad but God has already been here and He has prepared my way. There is deliverance and victory for me in this because God has blazed this trail ahead of me." That one scripture alone can change your entire life!

Psalm 1:1-3 is another passage I love:

How blessed is the man who does not walk in the counsel of the wicked, nor stand in the path of sinners, nor sit in the seat of scoffers! But his delight is in the law of the LORD, and in His law he meditates day and night. He will be like a tree firmly planted by streams of water, which yields its fruit in its season and its leaf does not wither; and in whatever he does, he prospers.

God says if you obey Him...if you meditate on His Word, learn His principles and try your best to adhere to them...you will be blessed. You will experience the abundant life Jesus Christ preached and provided. Your marriage will benefit, your children will grow up loving God and turn from rebellion. You will enjoy financial success. You will not have to read scores of books about how to feel good about yourself—you will feel good about yourself because you will have a right perspective of the person God created you to be. You will understand your purpose on earth and enjoy a fulfilling life.

If you are firmly rooted in the Word of God, when storms come, you will not despair. You will have hope and live in confidence that God is taking care of the future. You will be confident that He has provision and deliverance stored up for you. Your contribution to the situation is to wait on God. The Bible says when you wait on Him He works on your behalf. As you walk through crisis or trial you can rest in the fact that God is orchestrating events on your behalf. Since He has gone ahead of you, He has placed people and situations in strategic locations specifically for your benefit. In truth, it is a setup! God has set you up for victory. When all is said and done you will likely make Romans 10:11 your own by saying:

"I believed in God and I am not disappointed!"

Reasons NOT to Read the Bible

Ask any Christian if they believe reading the Bible is important and they will almost certainly answer emphatically, "Yes!" Yet in twenty plus years as a pastor...and even more as a Christian...I have heard just about every excuse that exists for *not* reading the Bible. A strong possibility exists that the first time I heard these reasons was when I used them myself!

Here are six of the most common reasons given for not reading the Bible—followed by my response to each:

1. "I'm just too busy."

Really? Guess what the number one moneymaking industry is in the United States? Leisure time activity! What does that tell us? We must have some *leisure time*! You and I are given 1,440 minutes every single day of our lives! Assuming we sleep for 8 hours each night, that leaves 960 minutes each day for working, driving, eating and everything else. Certainly we can spare 10 or 15 of those minutes to read the Bible. I want to challenge you to read just one or two chapters of the Bible each day. That is about what you will cover in 10 or 15 minutes. If you do that five days a week you will receive a life-changing return on your investment. Do the reading with your spouse and the dividends are even higher!

2.   "The Bible is too hard to understand."

Are you using the King James Bible that was written in 1611? Please get a modern version! If you have a New American Standard Bible and are having trouble understanding that, try a modern English version such as the New Living Bible or Today's English Version Bible. If you are a new Christian these may be especially helpful.   Eventually you will want a more literal translation but begin with a version you can enjoy reading. That is why these translations exist.

3.   "I can't remember what I read."

When my son was learning multiplication tables we used flash cards to help him memorize them because repetition is a valuable learning tool. Repetition works just as well for retaining scripture. The more you read the Word, the more it seeps in to your mind. I cannot count the times I have been talking with someone and a scripture and biblical principle comes to mind relating to our conversation. Often I do not know where the scripture is located in the Bible, but I know it is there because I have read it many times. Because I have been faithful to put the Word in my mind, the Holy Spirit is faithful to pull it out when I need it.

4.   "It's not practical for my life."

It is true that there are some areas of life that don't seem to be specifically mentioned in the Bible. Some examples are payroll expenses, bureaucracy, competition, deadlines, starting your own business and dealing with customers. If that is why you do not read the Bible I want to challenge you to read through the book of Proverbs three times. Get a notebook. As you read ask God to show you how these verses can be practically applied in your life. Begin to write down the ideas that come to you about applying these truths. I guarantee that if you do this you will see how practical God's Word really is.

5.   "The Bible is boring."

The Bible is anything but boring! Every conceivable aspect of human life is covered: romance, war, betrayal, intrigue, comedy, adventure, and redemption. In addition there are truths and principles that will improve your life. The key is to approach God's Word with expectation. Ask Him to speak to you and He *will!* Morning devotions cannot possibly be boring if the God who created the universe speaks to you through His Word.

I cannot tell you how often I have needed to make a decision or was struggling with something and God spoke to me about that specific thing *through His Word* during my morning devotions. When my church was faced with making a decision about our building God told me specifically what to do during my morning devotions as I read 2 Corinthians 8. I shared it with the church staff and board members and they recognized that it was direction from God about what we were to do. It confirmed other words He had spoken and we knew the direction God was taking us.

One of the most amazing instances of God speaking to me happened when I was 30 years old. After receiving my seminary degree I tried to start a church three separate times. Each time people around me said, "He's not ready." "He stutters! He can never be a preacher." "He does not have the anointing." The last attempt involved a Christian denomination that I'll not name. Some of the leaders decided that I was not ready but I had a different perspective. I thought, "How could I *not* be ready? I have spent the last eight years preparing for this very thing!"

I was living in my aunt's house at the time. I did not have a job because God would not allow me to work. I can see now that he needed to break the immense pride and arrogance I had in my life. Everywhere I went I encountered a divine setup! [I can personally attest to the fact that God goes ahead of us and prepares the way!] Without fail, I routinely would run into a former high school classmate or college friend who would tell me about their amazing success and then ask, "So Dave, what are you doing?" I was always perplexed how to answer. What I wanted to say was: "I'm unemployed, living off my aunt and I drive a Datsun truck which, thankfully, still runs! I've studied to be a Pastor and God has blessed my choice to live according to godly principles with the success that stands before you today!" I was humiliated! I used to tell God, "I would like to witness for you, but You have to give me something to witness about!"

When the leaders from that last denomination told me they could not support me in starting a church I was devastated. Before God called me to be a pastor I had been a high school teacher and football coach. I loved football! Coaching football was a passion, but I had to lay it down for God. When that final door slammed shut in my face I said, "Lord, if You are not going to use me then let me go back to doing what I love to do!" I was feeling so sorry for myself thinking that I had given up a great life for the Lord...only to be mistreated! "Lord, if this is the way you treat your people," I said, "You're lucky to have anybody at all!" I was feeling very low. The next morning during my devotions I read Acts 26:16:

"Get up and stand on your feet."

It was as though God was saying, "Dave, you sorry son of mine! Will you stop feeling sorry for yourself? Get up, get out of bed right now and wash your face. I should spank you. Get up!" I continued reading the scripture:

For this purpose I have appeared to you, to appoint you a minister and a witness.

The Holy Spirit fell on me at that moment. [This happened 15 years ago and I still choke up when I think about it.] I was so encouraged! I knew with certainty that God had just spoken to me and that He was going to use me. That would never have happened if I had not opened my Bible and read it.

The Bible says there is no partiality with God [Romans 2:11] so you can be certain He wants to do the same for you. God wants to speak to you! I like to imagine Jesus standing beside each believer saying, "Open the Word so I can talk to you. And I want you to talk to Me! Pray to Me and allow Me to respond to you through my Word."

6.   "I'm not motivated."

Do not blame God if you are lazy. Many people do nothing because they are waiting for a dramatic experience. Perhaps they expect a bolt of lightning to split the sky and God's thundering voice to say, "Go sign up to help in the Children's Ministry." God is certainly free to do that, but He usually does not choose to speak that way. I agree with our dear friend Bill Wilson who says, "Most of what I've done in my life is just because I saw a need and I said, 'Here am I Lord, send me.'"

Why Godly Fear Requires Reading

There are four fundamental reasons why reading the Bible is mandatory if you desire to Fear the Lord:

1.   To gain knowledge of God's perspective.

Knowing what God has done in the past...His promises, His warnings, what He expects from you...will help you make decisions and plan for the future. The more you read the Word of God the more it washes you and gives you a godly perspective on your life. So often when we go through difficulties, especially if we are immature in our Christianity, we focus on the circumstance and not on what God might be doing through it. Reading the Word lifts those blinders and enables us to see from God's perspective. Then we approach the circumstance with faith, "This looks bad, Lord, but I know You are going to deliver me. You delivered me in the past and I have read about others in the Bible that You miraculously delivered. You promised never to leave or forsake me so I know I am safe in Your care through this situation."

Having God's perspective makes all the difference in the world. Without it we are more likely to say, "My life is over! Everything is ruined! This is hopeless!"

A Christian named Terry Anderson was held captive in Lebanon for more than 6 years. By his own admission he rarely read the Bible before he was kidnapped. When he was finally freed he said, "Constantly over the years of captivity I found consolation and counsel in the Bible. I read it over 50 times. It was an enormous help to me." Why? He acquired God's perspective on his situation! He knew his captors might kill him at any time but reading the Bible caused him to understand that it would only be death to his body, not his soul or spirit. He knew he would be in a much better place. The Apostle Paul said,

To live is Christ and to die is gain.

[Philippians 1:21]

God wants to reveal His perspective for your life. He wants to answer your questions such as, "What should I do? What is happening? What good can possibly come from this? What is the purpose in this situation? How should I respond? What is Your plan in this God?" The most content and joy-filled Christians are those who have a godly perspective on their life and circumstances. Even during times of trial or crisis they focus on what God is doing, not on what is happening. Crisis is simply a bump in the road. That level of peace is only available when you have the Lord's perspective.

People are really good at thinking about themselves and the negative. I am an expert in this area. My wife, Mary, can attest to the fact that in any situation I am able to figure out every negative possibility in less than thirty seconds. It comes naturally to me, yet I must choose to fight my natural inclination and walk in the spirit. I must decide to block the barrage of negative ideas and choose to trust God's sovereignty in the situation. I have the power to choose what I will think! We must decide to say, "This is a small thing. In two years it will not be a tragedy, it will be a testimony of God's protection, provision, or deliverance."

When you pursue God's perspective, problems that seemed huge in the past become small. The peace that accompanies God's perspective is available to everyone but is only enjoyed by those who choose to read His Word.

2. To know what we believe.

Behavior is always driven by beliefs and convictions. If you swerve to avoid walking under a ladder, at some level you believe that luck and ladders have power over what happens to you.

When you read the Bible you come to *know* what God says. As you accept His Word you develop beliefs and convictions based on His truth and your actions change.

Several years ago when Mary and I were having marriage problems, she could not stand me and I was convinced that her upbringing was the root of our problems. Tensions between us became so bad that I called the man who leads our marriage ministry. I explained to Mike that my wife's emotional problems were destroying our marriage and something had to be done. To my surprise I discovered that one of Mary's biggest marriage problems was me! Today Mary and I have a solid marriage and a good home life. My willingness to call for help was the direct result of strong convictions I have about marriage that are drawn directly from the Word of God.

My father was a pastor but his real gift was marriage counseling. He told me that in 42 years of counseling not one couple with a deep commitment to the Lord divorced—even when it was evident that they despised one another! Their convictions about covenant resulted in a firm resolve *against* divorce. Faithfulness to their covenant was rewarded and they enjoyed a deeper love for one another than they had before the problems. *Covenant* is the key! Something wonderful and supernatural happens in a marriage when the covenant is honored and the couple works through extreme difficulties. Each is refined in the process, and their capacity to love each other increases.

That is exactly what happened when Mary and I worked through our marriage difficulties. She was willing to examine herself and make changes and I did the same. When we pointed accusing fingers at ourselves instead of each other, God was able to do some wonderful things in each of us. Knowing what we believed helped us identify faulty thinking and changed our behavior.

People often use the Bible incorrectly, and if you do not know what it says...what *you* believe...you cannot help guide them to truth. A young man I know who attends San Diego State University recognized that one of the books used in his religion class presented false teaching about Christianity. He began taking his Bible to class to expose the inaccuracies. Because he is faithful to read the Word of God, others had an opportunity to know the truth about the Bible.

Holding to biblical convictions can save relationships but the absence of them can destroy lives. A recent example involves a mother who drowned her five children. A jury found her guilty of capital murder and she was sentenced to life in prison. Her family members and representatives of a special interest organization were outraged. They claimed prosecutors were merciless to bring capital murder charges against a mentally ill woman over-whelmed by the demands of motherhood.

At the time this horrific event made news, there was a woman in my church who just gave birth to her eighth child! My father was one of seven children and his family was unusually small compared to most in his hometown of Ashley, North Dakota. Years ago, when America's economy was based in agriculture, the prevailing attitude was, "The more children you have the more farm hands you have!" Many families had ten or twelve children.

The Bible says God will *not* give you more than you can handle, yet this woman decided that having five children was unbearable and killing them was her only option. Worse still, her husband... the father of those children...said he and other family members were *offended* that she was prosecuted at all!

When I read the news article containing his statements I could not believe it! The Bible is clear: each person is responsible for his or her actions. That is the foundational message of the cross! The world makes every effort to deny the existence of sin because without it there is no responsibility! The woman had postpartum depression; while this is serious, it certainly is no excuse to kill your children. She had a terrible childhood. Many people, including relatives of the murdered children, argued that those conditions produced something in her she could not control, so she was not responsible. Essentially they are trying to deny the existence of sin and release sinners from responsibility for their sin. That mother murdered her children and the Bible is clear— murder is a sin! Should compassion and mercy be shown to this woman? Absolutely! She desperately needs Jesus.

According to Deuteronomy 24:16 each person is responsible for their own sin. Romans 14:10 states that all will stand before the judgment seat of Christ. 2 Corinthians 5:10 says all will be judged for their deeds. Every person is responsible for his or her actions! That is the reason Jesus came to earth and died a sinner's death. Responsibility for sin was not waived—it was assumed by Christ and the debt was paid!

People who have bought into the argument that the mother was not responsible for what she did to her children may be shocked by the truths of scripture about her actions. Their perspective shocks me because I know what the Word of God says about murder!

Modern culture encourages the spreading of opinion. Often people simply adopt the most popular philosophy of the day. Just ask someone why he or she opposes a particular politician or supports a certain issue and you are likely to find that they themselves do not know! They are simply parroting whatever is popular. Christians need to know what they believe and be prepared to share the truth found in God's Word.

3.   To get the most out of life.

Why do so many people today have marital problems, depression, rebellious children, financial difficulties, addictions and other weighty troubles? Usually it is because they have disobeyed the Word of God. Living victoriously comes from being washed regularly by God's Word. The Bible is clear that if you align yourself with God you will enjoy a prosperous life. It contains strategies for raising godly children, enjoying a good marriage and living successfully. Joshua 1:8 says,

This book of the law shall not depart from your mouth, but you shall meditate on it day and night, so that you may be careful to do according to all that is written in it; for then you will make your way prosperous, and then you will have success.

At the beginning of this chapter I described what I call the formula for failure. Now I want to share the **recipe for success**:

113

1] **Memorize the Word of God.** Memorize it so that when you need a scripture, a promise or a biblical principle it is readily available to you.

2] **Read and study God's Word**. As you do, ask Him how it applies to your life. God will change you in the process.

3] **Obey what you read**. No matter what it costs—obey! Friend, you will never be sorry. Whoever believes God and trusts Him enough to do as He says will never be disappointed. [Romans 10:11]

4. To be a witness for Christ.

2 Corinthians 5:17-20 essentially says all Christians have a ministry of reconciliation. Once we are reconciled to God through Jesus, we are to be a witness for Jesus so that others may be reconciled to God. If you and I do not proclaim the truth about Jesus who will? The world is full of false ideas about God, Jesus, and life after death. Satan is anxious to exploit those ideas. Some false ideas are palatable to the masses because they alleviate responsibility for sin while others embrace sinful pursuits. These "truths" are simply age-old lies perpetrated by the father of lies. The only truths that have the power to save and change lives are the ones contained in the Word of God. If you and I do not know what it says and share those truths with the people around us, it simply will not be done. Yet the more you and I study the Bible the better equipped we are with a relevant response to society's problems, concerns, and faulty philosophies.

When you learn godly principles and make yourself available to God, I guarantee you will have opportunities to witness for Christ. People are interested in what the Bible says. Just tell an unbeliever that you read and believe the Bible and they will ask questions.

"What about this?"
"How do you explain that?"
"What about that?"

Be prepared! They may laugh, scoff or become angry, but you are being given a golden opportunity to share the Word of God with someone who desperately needs it...whether they know it or not. God frequently woos non-believers to Himself through just such encounters. Each is a small part of His greater plan to draw the person into a relationship with Jesus. Whenever you speak God's Word it releases power that *always* accomplishes something. It convicts. It enlightens. It encourages. It exposes the heart.

So will My word be which goes forth from My mouth; it will not return to Me empty, without accomplishing what I desire, and without succeeding in the matter for which I sent it. [Isaiah 55:11]

It is never a waste of breath to speak God's Word. It always accomplishes exactly what He intends.

The Final Authority

Who or what has final authority over your life? Are your decisions based on your feelings, your ideas, or a book you read? Are your beliefs grounded in something you saw on Oprah Winfrey, a college professor's philosophy, or the most socially acceptable opinions of the day?

The modern trend is for each person to be his or her own god—establishing their own rules and doing exactly as they desire! Is that your choice? Or do you submit yourself to God and His Word...reading it...washing your mind with it...allowing Him to be your final authority?

When you base your life on the truth you know from reading the Word of God, you reap the benefits of fearing the Lord.

CHAPTER SEVEN

The Importance of Prayer
for Those Who Fear The Lord

You do not have because you do not ask. *[James 4:2]*

What place does prayer occupy in the life of a person who chooses to fear God? Martin Luther once said,

Prayer is the most important thing in my life.
If I should neglect prayer for even a single day I
would lose the fire of faith.

Prayer is central in the life of anyone who chooses to fear God. Luther understood its importance because he knew the impact it had on his faith. Hebrews 11:6 states that it is impossible to please God without faith, and no wonder! Faith is simply trusting God's Word above everything else—then acting on it! A person with faith obeys God despite what he can see, hear, touch, think, understand or experience.

Luther described his faith as a fire, but it was not always so. Faith of that magnitude does not happen overnight—it happens over time—and prayer is the kindling that sparks the flame. Like everyone who chooses to have faith in God, Luther took a chance. He dared to believe that God's Word is true—God really does hear and respond to prayer [Psalm 145:18-19].

Luther prayed and God's response fueled his faith. Each miraculous answer to prayer caused Luther's trust in God to grow. Over time the flicker of faith became a roaring flame that was unquenchable by even the most difficult circumstances. Luther knew the only thing that could extinguish the fire of his faith was a day without prayer.

The recipe for faith is the same today...you pray, God responds. The longer you pray the more you experience God's faithfulness and the more you grow to trust Him. When you trust God you are willing to depend on His truth instead of your understanding or experience. Your faith grows as you look back and see incident after incident of God answering your prayers. You learn that He can handle *anything* you bring to Him, so your expectations rise and you invite Him to do even greater things.

God *loves* that kind of faith from His people! He loves it when you trust Him completely—and it all begins with prayer! Prayer is the foundation of an intimate, trusting relationship with God.

You Do Not Have Because You Do Not Ask!

My favorite scripture regarding prayer is James 4:2. Inspired by the Holy Spirit, James wrote:

You do not have because you do not ask.

I believe these nine little words explain why so many Christians feel discouraged and are defeated by things that God would gladly give them victory over if only they would ask!

If you do not ask God to release His power in your life, generally speaking, it will not happen. You may be a born-again believer, but if you are not seeking God's help and guidance you are missing out on more blessing than you can imagine. Often I hear Christians ask,

"Why can't I gain victory over this issue?"
"Why am I so easily discouraged?"
"Where is God's power in my life?"

Church staff and ministry leaders ask...

"Why aren't our programs working?"
"Why aren't more people being saved?"
"Why do so many Christians live without convictions or tolerate sin?"
"Why isn't the Spirit of God more powerful when we come together?"

I believe the answer to all those questions is:

You do not have, because you do not ask.

Many people are quick to accuse God of not helping them, yet they rarely consult Him or invite His participation in what they do.

Though it is well disguised, the root of the problem is often pride. Prayer humbles you before God. It acknowledges His sovereignty, essentially saying, "You are God and I am not. You are perfectly in control of my life and this situation. You are powerful enough to work even the most terrible situation for my good."

Humble yourselves in the presence of the Lord, and He will exalt you. [James 4:10]

Imagine that—the almighty, omnipotent Creator of the Universe will exalt *you* if only you will humble yourself before Him and pray.

Prayer Is *NOT* Optional if You Fear God!

Prayer is not optional if you desire to fear God. In fact, prayer is the beginning of fearing the Lord! One facet of fearing God is trusting Him and you must put that trust into action by being a man or woman of prayer.

Friends, family, society—even fellow Christians and your own mind at times—will tell you not to do what God wants you to do. You will make wrong choices if you are not asking God to guide you. If you want to live a victorious life in Jesus Christ...able to overcome any obstacle...you must develop the discipline of prayer.

I am not saying you must spend hours each day in prayer, but you do need to develop the discipline of praying every day.

My brother, Mark, and I have a group of people in our church who have a gift of prayer. These people have a gift of praying. They set out to pray and an hour later they are still in prayer. The Lord wakes them in the middle of the night and they pray for three or four hours. Prayer seems to come easily for these brothers and sisters. It comes easily because God has given them a special gift of intercessory prayer.

Not so for me! Developing the discipline of daily prayer has been a struggle—it seems something always gets in the way. I expect that it will be a lifelong struggle for me but it is one I will endure because I want God's power, strength, wisdom, and anointing in my life and that only comes through prayer.

Americans typically do not like the word *discipline*. It sounds like—and is—work! I believe one reason the Spirit of God moves so freely in Asian countries like Korea is because their culture values discipline. It is emphasized and expected...children are taught to live disciplined lives and they grow into disciplined adults.

When Korean Christians pray they have the same disciplined approach as with everything else and the result is consistent prayer. There are Prayer Mountains in Korea where thousands of people pray day and night. Church leaders ask people to pray, they comply in a highly disciplined manner, and the Holy Spirit moves in power.

The majority of American Christians lack discipline. What would happen in our country...in our cities and neighborhoods...if believers disciplined themselves to pray? I long for the day we see the answer to that question...when God's people rally together to invite Him to move in power in America.

Prayer is vital in the believer's life because it is the only thing that releases God's power, influence, wisdom and anointing. Prayer turns the impossible into the *probable*. Miraculous things happen because the Holy Spirit can accomplish through your prayers what would be impossible for you on your own.

The Power of God's Presence!

Prayer is not optional if you want the power of God in your life. Born-again, heaven-bound believers who do not seek God daily in prayer do not enjoy His presence or experience His power. Essentially they are choosing to live under their own power, and that is no power at all!

When you prayerfully invite God to guide you and govern your life, you tap into His power, protection, and provision.

Consider it in these terms: an electric appliance requires a current to function. Inserting the plug into an electric outlet accesses the current. In the life of a Christian, prayer is the equivalent of plugging into *God's current!* It is what releases His power to and through His people. Just as an appliance is useless without the power of an electrical current, so a Christian's life is powerless without accessing God's current through prayer.

Jesus said,

> *I am the vine, you are the branches; he who abides in Me, and I in him, he bears much fruit; for apart from Me you can do nothing. If you abide in Me, and My words abide in you, ask whatever you wish, and it shall be done for you. [John 15:5, 7]*

Abiding in Jesus...seeking His presence and His will...produces fruit in your life. That fruit is essentially the manifestation of God's power and provision. A consistent prayer life provides God with an avenue to demonstrate His miraculous works, which is a testimony to the world that Jesus Christ is real, relevant, and in relationship with ordinary people.

My brother, John, and his wife, Gina, are a good example of this Kingdom truth. They had a neighbor whose income was about three times more than theirs. One day the neighbor said, "I can't believe you guys! You go on vacation, you own your own home, God just does things for you all the time." The neighbor was amazed by God's generous provision for them despite their income. Through prayer and obedience to God's Word, John and Gina invited God's power and provision. The display of His goodness and generosity to them was a testimony to this unbelieving neighbor.

Prayer Opens Doors

While imprisoned in Rome the Apostle Paul wrote these instructions to the Colossians:

Devote yourselves to prayer, keeping alert in it with an attitude of thanksgiving; praying at the same time for us as well, that God will open up to us a door for the Word, so that we may speak forth the mystery of Christ, for which I have also been imprisoned; that I may make it clear in the way I ought to speak. [Colossians 4:2-4]

Paul is essentially saying, "Pray for me! I want God's influence and power, through His Spirit, to open doors so I can preach the Gospel." Paul knew the power of prayer in the most impossible of circumstances.

When you pray about tough situations you can be certain that the end is not yet written. Prayer *will* make a difference! It opens doors and invites God to perform miracles on your behalf.

In preparation for this chapter I sought testimonies from members of my church staff. I went to Children's Pastor, Dan Deyling, and asked, "Dan, what is the first testimony that comes to your mind of God opening a door for you because you prayed?"

Dan replied, "Well the first thing that comes to my mind happened about ten years ago. I was laid off from my construction job and you and Mark offered me a job one day a week."

"The construction company called shortly after that and asked me to come back to work for them. I asked if I could work four days a week so I could keep working one day at the church but they said no."

"My wife, Darcy, and I had to make a decision. Was God calling us into the ministry or should I go back to construction? We believed that God wanted me to stay on at the church so we went to Him in prayer, 'God, you are going to have to open doors for us. We will continue working at church one day a week to try to start a children's ministry but You are going to have to provide for us because the church doesn't have the money to support us right now.'"

"So every time a bill came we would get on our knees and pray, 'Lord, open a door!' Each time, without fail, a side job would come up. I did not advertise that I was doing side work and the church was small then so there wasn't a lot of work coming from the church members. These jobs were coming from people who just called to ask if I still did carpentry work. For more than a year I got enough side work to pay all the bills and stay in the ministry."

Eventually God prospered our church enough to make Dan a fulltime staff member able to support his family on the income he earns doing God's work. The Children's Ministry Dan believed God wanted him to begin now serves hundreds of children each week. God opened doors of provision and ministry because Dan and Darcy prayed.

Dan's story was so encouraging I wanted more, so I walked across the hall to the office of Dan's brother, Jim, who is Pastor of Discipleship and Small Groups at our church. I asked Jim the same question I had asked Dan.

"Christmas!" Jim replied. He explained that a couple of years earlier at Christmas time he had a financially difficult month...vehicles broke down and there were other unexpected drains on his income. His Christmas budget was small but he deeply desired to continue his family's Christmas tradition of blessing a needy family with groceries and gifts. Jim and his wife, Melanie, scraped together forty dollars to spend on a family they knew had great need. It would not buy much but they were determined to give.

They went to a grocery warehouse and filled the cart with economy items like macaroni and cheese. Suddenly Jim sensed an inner prodding from God, "If you are giving this food in the name of Jesus shouldn't you be giving the best?" Jim and Melanie agreed they should, so they unloaded the economy items and piled the cart high with choice foods and gifts.

Jim prayed, "Lord, we will have to pay for this with the money set aside for our Christmas, but I trust that You will open a door because I know You really want us to bless this family."

When they took the cart to the checkout a woman stepped in line behind them. She examined the bounty in their cart and said, "Boy, you're really stocking up for the holidays!" Jim replied that it was not for his family, then explained their Christmas tradition of blessing a family with great need. The woman began to cry. Jim thought, "I'm going to get to witness to this lady! God, I am ready!" Instead, the woman did not want to talk. Jim waited for the Holy Spirit's release to witness to her, but nothing happened!

The cashier finished ringing up the items and announced the total...almost two hundred dollars! As Jim reached for his checkbook the woman behind him spoke, "You're not going to pay for that, I am!" Tears were streaming down her cheeks as she addressed the clerk, "Sir, you do not take the money from him. Here it is!" She paid for everything Jim and Melanie had placed in the cart! They walked out of the store praising the Lord for miraculously answering Jim's prayer! Miracles like that just seem to happen when you pray.

The Most Important Part of Parenting

Every parent knows that raising children is a tough job. You can read enough "How To" books to fill a library but it will never match the benefits of one humble prayer for help when a crisis hits.

During elementary school, my son, Andy, was having trouble learning to read at one point...he was a grade or two behind the rest of his class. Mary and I had him tested to see if there was a major problem, but the results showed there was no dyslexia, only slow processing skills. We concluded that we simply started him in school a little too early.

Our children attend the school started by our church, Venture Christian School. Students at Venture spend two or three days per week in class and their days off—home schooling. We took a two-week vacation in beautiful Montana so during that time our children did only home schooling.

Our return home meant that Andy would be going back to the classroom but he did not want to go! He cried, "Please, please, Daddy, I don't want to go! Please, I don't want to go there. Can I just home school all the time? Please?"

If the issue were simply that he did not want to go to school there would be no discussion but I was concerned that his reading problem was prompting this protest. I suspected that he was embarrassed about it around the other students. I did not know what to do, so I told my son that his mother and I would pray about his proposition, but he had to start back to school.

Andy went to school and I prayed throughout the entire day. "Lord," I pleaded, "You better give me an answer here because I am clueless!"

I know I can trust God's Word for guidance in all things, but there is no scripture that specifically says, "If your child is having difficulty reading and does not want to attend school, do *this*."

I honestly did not know how to handle this dilemma, but I knew it had to begin with prayer. I came home from work that day and said, "Andy, I want to talk to you." "Sure, Dad," he replied, and we stepped into my home office where we could talk privately. We both sat down, but before I spoke a single word he said, "Dad, I thought about it and I'll go to school for the rest of the year and then we'll talk about it." "Ok," I said and he stood up and walked out of the room.

I sat there for a moment dumbfounded, but I knew this was the result of God responding to my prayer.

The most important part of parenting is partnering with God! Parenting is easy when you lean on the Holy Spirit because miracles like the one with Andy happen all the time. If I had not prayed that day I would have come home stressed, depending on Mary and myself to find an answer. Instead, God took care of the problem...crisis over!

Prayer is the Battleground!

Prayer is the real battleground of our world. When God's people understand that and wage war through prayer, lives are changed, loved ones are saved, marriages are restored, financial miracles occur, and people accomplish things far beyond their own abilities.

Prayer is the most important factor in seeking God's will and it is vital if you want to experience His supernatural involvement in your life. You invite God's power, anointing, wisdom and provision when you submit to His authority and become a man or woman who wages war through prayer.

Psalm 109 is one of my favorite passages on prayer because it shows the depth of King David's trust in God.

> *O God of my praise, do not be silent! For they have opened the wicked and deceitful mouth against me; they have spoken against me with a lying tongue. They have also surrounded me with words of hatred, and fought against me without cause. In return for my love they act as my accusers; but I am in prayer. [Psalm 109:1-4]*

In the face of adversity David prayed. The circumstances, though perilous, did not rob him of hope and expectation because he had battled with prayer as his weapon before and witnessed the powerful response of God.

God delivered David by guiding a single smooth stone into the skull of a giant and gave him the ability and accuracy to take down ferocious beasts. David had experienced God's power and protection and he believed God would deliver him again...he expected that God had something good in store for him...so he prayed.

But David did not just pray when he was in peril. Read through the Psalms and you will see scores of passages that are David's prayers of praise, thanksgiving, and worship. The man simply loved God and loved communicating with Him! Can you think of a better weapon to use against Satan?

A Commitment to Prayer

If you were to graph the prayer life of many Christians you would find a series of peaks and valleys: a few peaks of intense prayer and long valleys of prayerlessness.

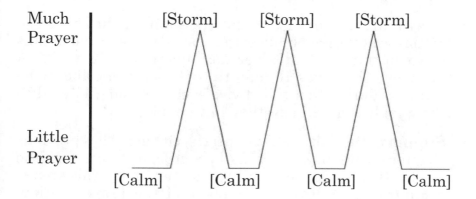

Most of the peaks represent times when storms are raging. The boss says, "You're fired!" or the school nurse calls and says there is a strange lump on your child's neck. There is a significant peak in prayer for most believers during storms but when Jesus calms the storm through His provision, healing, deliverance, or peace, prayer often sinks into a valley of near nothingness.

This sad pattern was true in my life and in the lives of so many people I encountered in the church. This pattern prompted one of the most powerful ministries at Foothills Christian Fellowship—the Prayer Society.

The Prayer Society is a group of people who commit to making prayer a priority. It was established to help develop the discipline of daily prayer and to invite God into every area of our church. Prayer Society members make a five-fold commitment:

- **Attend church regularly:** Members who regularly attend church are more likely to pray for the church and its ministries. They feel more a part of what god is doing and have opportunities to see Him answer their prayers.

127

- **Pray through special prayer lists:** Two lists per month are sent to members, each containing a dozen or so prayer requests. Members are to pray for each item on the list at least once. The Prayer Society was founded to help believers develop a discipline of prayer—these lists encourage that discipline.

- **Pray a minimum of 2 1/2 hours each week:** This block of time was chosen because it is easy to achieve and breaks down to thirty minutes per day, five days per week. A member who drives 15 minutes between work and home can pray during that time twice each day and easily fulfill the weekly commitment they have made.

- **Support the church through tithes:** The previous chapter on finances explains how crucial it is to fear the Lord with our finances. Failure to obey God in this area is a *hindrance* to prayer. Members of the Prayer Society must be in obedience to God with their finances.

- **Daily striving for holiness and obedience to God:** Willful disobedience in any area of life is a hindrance to prayer. Members of the Prayer Society who desire to fear God in their prayer lives must strive to obey Him daily.

The Prayer Society has been an immense success at Foothills. If a member of the church can be involved in only one ministry, this is the one I ask that they participate in because it is the most important. Prayer is the beginning of everything in the Kingdom of God, so if a believer can commit to only one activity it should be prayer!

Each year Foothills offers senior high school and junior high school camps that have proven to be very successful, because hundreds of people are praying for the youth involved in these ministries. God loves those prayers and responds by pouring out His Spirit on our kids. It is awesome!

When Foothills hosts evangelical programs they, too, are successful because so many are praying.

At this writing, there are over 500 members in the Prayer Society. It has been one of the most powerful factors in realizing my dream to see God move in our church and in the East County of San Diego.

The Prayer Society has been one of the most powerful tools for building consistency in my personal prayer life and it has helped hundreds of God's people develop the discipline of communing with Him daily.

Persevering in Prayer

Jesus certainly knew the value of consistent prayer, and He taught His followers to persevere in it.

Then He said to them, "Suppose one of you has a friend, and goes to him at midnight and says to him, 'Friend, lend me three loaves; for a friend of mine has come to me from a journey, and I have nothing to set before him'; and from inside he answers and says, 'Do not bother me; the door has already been shut and my children and I are in bed; I cannot get up and give you anything.' I tell you, even though he will not get up and give him anything because he is his friend, yet because of his persistence he will get up and give him as much as he needs. So I say to you, ask, and it will be given to you; seek, and you will find; knock, and it shall be opened to you. For everyone who asks, receives; and he who seeks, finds; and to him who knocks, it will be opened." [Luke 11:5-10]

Jesus was instructing them to follow His example and develop a daily prayer life with God. He knew His followers would encounter struggles and wanted them to understand that perseverance is essential for victory.

Years ago it was common for people to use the phrase "praying through." If a believer had a struggle or need, they would pray through the issue until God's response was apparent.

Today, it is more common for believers to give up than to pray through. They pray about something and when the answer is not immediately evident, they stop praying. Often these people spend the rest of their lives believing God did not answer their prayer. That is not what happened...they gave up too soon!

God *always* answers persistent, persevering prayer. Many times a battle must be won in the heavenly realm or bondages must be broken before the answer is seen in the natural. Jesus said if you persevere in prayer you *will* receive an answer. His words were very clear and deliberate:

> *Ask, and it **will** be given to you; seek, and you **will** find; knock, and it **shall be** opened to you. For **everyone** who asks, receives; and he who seeks, finds; and to him who knocks, it will be opened. [Matthew 7:2-8]*

There are no maybes in His message! If you ask you will receive. It is not reserved for an elite group. Answered prayer is for everyone who asks!

Discipline Provides Power to Persevere

One of the many benefits of a disciplined prayer life is that when your flesh grows tired of praying for something and you are tempted to give up, you press on because prayer has become a habit. You have developed in yourself the power to persevere!

There are things I continue to pray about simply because they appear on the list I pray over daily. Without the habit of daily prayer [and my list to remind me] chances are I would act on my feelings and give up.

One example is my prayer for the salvation of my brother, Tim. He is my only sibling who is not saved. I have been praying for him for years, but I know I would have become discouraged and quit if I did not have the habit of daily prayer and a list with his name on it. Instead, I persevere and know it is only a matter of time before I shall see the tangible answer God has already given in response to my request.

Perseverance Prevents Discouragement

You have seen the importance of persevering to gain victory, yet there is a second reason Jesus encourages His followers to persevere in prayer:

> *Now He was telling them a parable to show that at all times they ought to pray and not to lose heart, saying, "In a certain city there was a judge who did not fear God and did not respect man. There was a widow in that city, and she kept coming to him, saying, 'Give me legal protection from my opponent.' For a while he was unwilling; but afterward he said to himself, 'Even though I do not fear God nor respect man, yet because this widow bothers me, I will give her legal protection, otherwise by continually coming she will wear me out.'" And the Lord said, "Hear what the unrighteous judge said; now, will not God bring about justice for His elect who cry to Him day and night, and will He delay long over them? I tell you that He will bring about justice for them quickly. However, when the Son of Man comes, will He find faith on the earth?"*
> [Luke 18:1-8]

Verse one reveals the second reason—to *prevent discouragement!* Think about that for a moment...a believer is either praying or discouraged! If you do not pray you will be defeated. If you do not pray, God's power will not be released to operate on your behalf. Either you develop the discipline of prayer and involve yourself in a consistent relationship with Jesus Christ or you live in discouragement!

The Secret to Developing the Discipline of Prayer

What is the secret to developing the discipline of daily prayer? It certainly is not based in feelings—there are many days you do not *feel* like praying. It cannot depend on circumstances—you will pray during the storms but when things run smoothly you will not be motivated to pray.

I have learned that there are two essential elements to successfully developing the discipline of prayer:

1.   You must determine a specific time.
2.   You must determine a specific place.

Jesus refers to these two essential elements in Matthew 6:6:

When you pray, go into your inner room, close your door, and pray to your Father who is in secret, and your Father who sees what is done in secret will reward you.

First, He addresses having a specific time to pray...He said **when** you pray not **if** you pray! Prayer was a daily priority to Jesus and He expected it to be a priority with His followers.

If you want to establish a discipline of prayer you *must* schedule a specific time each day that you commit to praying. It does not matter if you choose to pray at six o'clock in the morning, during your drive between home and work, or just before bedtime. You may decide to spend fifteen, twenty or thirty minutes in prayer—that is up to you. The critical element is that you schedule a specific time each day to be with God and *keep that appointment*!

Simply planning to pray *sometime* during the day does not work. There will always be something to derail your plans and prevent you from making time to pray. Establishing a specific time for prayer makes it a priority in your schedule and insures that it will be a consistent part of your day.

Second, Jesus instructed His followers to go into their inner room and shut the door. It is essential to have a special place where you can go each day at your appointed prayer time. It may be your bathroom, living room, car, office, backyard, garage, or any other place you can go to be alone with your Father.

The key is having a set place to sit with God.

It is important to protect the time you spend with God in prayer. Members of your family should know that when you go into your prayer closet you are not available!

Perhaps you are familiar with the story of John Wesley's mother—she had so many children there was not one place in her home where she could be alone to pray, but there was a specific place she went. Her children knew that she was not to be disturbed while she was in prayer. She would sit down in a chair in the middle of her bustling home and fling her apron over her head. Even the youngest child knew that when mother was sitting in the chair under her apron she must be left alone...or else!

Friend, I am thoroughly convinced that this is the only way you will develop the discipline of consistent, persevering prayer. Over the years I have talked to many people who have mastered daily prayer and every one of them scheduled a specific time and had a specific place for prayer. They are following Jesus' model:

> *Very early in the morning, while it was still dark, Jesus got up, left the house and went off to a solitary place, where he prayed. [Mark 1:35]*

Reap the Rewards of a Good Habit!

Have you developed the discipline of daily prayer? Is it possible that *"you do not have because you do not ask"*? If you do not consistently seek God you are not accessing all He has for you. If you are not persevering in prayer you are missing out on miracles He is willing to perform on your behalf.

Prayer is not optional if you desire to experience God's presence and power. Prayer must be central in your life if you choose to fear and obey Him.

If you have developed the discipline of daily prayer—excellent! You know its value and no doubt live victoriously despite the circumstances that come your way. But if you are not making prayer a daily priority, accept that His mercies are new every morning and begin fresh today. He longs to listen to the things that are in your heart and on your mind.

Schedule a time and place *right now* that you will sit in the presence of your loving Savior each day. It will be the beginning of a good and rewarding habit!

CHAPTER EIGHT

Fearing the Lord Involves Respecting God's Delegated Authority

In this chapter we are going to answer the question, "If I choose to fear God, how does that affect how I treat, respond, or react to God's delegated authority in the church?" This chapter will not cover authority in any other area beside that of the Church.

Understanding spiritual authority is vital to the well-being of the church. One of the main reasons why many pastors leave their churches is because they grow weary of all the criticism, dissention, fault-finding and constant questioning over every decision they make. I know a man who recently stepped down from the ministry simply because he became weary of all the questioning. People contested every decision he made.

This chapter is vital for the area of discipleship, and is not triggered by any problem in our own church. In my years as a pastor, I have always felt support from our church members. Whenever Mark and I have felt God has given us a vision to go a certain direction, we have felt the loving support from the church.

Unfortunately, that is not true in many other churches.

What a blessing our church was when we decided to try to buy the El Cajon Towne Center. We invited our church to come and pray with us when we went before the El Cajon City Council. So many of our church showed up that we had no room to put them all! That was one of the most encouraging moments in my life of being a pastor.

As I share this, I do not want anybody to get the impression that they should blindly follow a minister or church leader. Instead, it is all about your heart attitude. When most people become part of a church, they say, "The Lord led me to this church." When they acknowledge that the Lord led them to a group of believers, they are also submitting to God's spiritual authority that He has placed in that church.

In the church, God has given a spiritual authority to those placed in position of leadership. We need to respect and submit to them, making sure we are not a hindrance to what God is trying to do through them.

Satan wants to cause division. God has ordained that He is going to reach the world and minister to the world through the Church. Satan wants to do anything he can to neutralize the Church's ability to do that. One of his strategies is to find willing participants in the church who will sow seeds of dissention, discord and distrust, especially against church leadership. If a church refuses to follow and support their leaders, that church will never accomplish much in their community.

Satan's greatest weapon is to neutralize the local congregation by encouraging members to question and criticize all levels of leadership so the church will become side tracked, and sapped of the necessary energy to pursue its ministry.

Finally, questioning authority can lead to rebellion in a church. Rebellion is rooted in pride and an unwillingness to live humbly before God. Rebellion against all delegated authority, government and spiritual, exposes a heart not yielded before God.

The real danger I have seen over the years is that people who sow discord and distrust toward leadership do it with religiosity and a purported concern for the church. I know this because I did everything I could in my early ministry to subvert a pastor's authority [more about that later in this chapter].

So often people's criticism of leadership is clothed in religious concerns. For example, "The Spirit of God really wants to move here. If only the pastor would allow us to _____ [you fill in the blank]. We need to pray for our pastor so that he hears the Spirit of God."

That type of attitude causes mistrust and dissention in the church. If you are doing that now, or have done it in the past, you are playing into Satan's hands! The people of God must become united behind our spiritual leaders so we can do damage to the kingdom of darkness! I believe one of the reasons that our own church reaches 2,500[+] children and youth a week is because our congregation has stood squarely behind Mark and I and said, "Let's go!" If many in our church would have instead decided to say, "That is not going to happen, God's leading us in a different direction; besides we don't want a bunch of kids causing damage around here," we would not have the children's and youth ministries we have today.

It is important for Christians to submit themselves to the delegated authority in whatever church they go to. When you decide to commit to a church you do it voluntarily believing God has called you to that church. The next step is to then voluntarily submit yourself to the spiritual authority that God has installed in that church!

Spiritual Authority Gives Us Informed Direction

Printed below is an actual radio conversation between the British and the Irish off the coast of Ireland. The transcript was released by the Chief of Naval Operations on October 10, 1998.

Irish: *Please divert your course 15 degrees to the south to avoid a collision.*

British: *Recommend <u>you</u> divert your course 15 degrees to the north to avoid a collision.*

Irish: *Negative. You will have to divert your course 15 degrees to the south to avoid a collision.*

British: *This is the Captain of a British Navy Ship. I say again, divert your course!*

Irish: *Negative. I say again you will have to divert your course or there will be a collision!*

British: *This is the Aircraft Carrier HMS Britannia, the second largest ship in the British Atlantic fleet; 3 destroyers, 3 cruisers and numerous support vessels accompany us. I demand you change your course 15 degrees north, I say again, 15 degrees north, or countermeasures will be undertaken to ensure the safety of this ship.*

Irish: *We are a lighthouse...your call.*

When we try to usurp or undermine spiritual authority it is as ridiculous as that navy captain trying to move the obstacle of a lighthouse that was in his path.   God has set up spiritual authority, and it is His delegated authority in the Church.   He is the one who created it, and has placed government in His church.

For this reason I left you in Crete, that you might set in order what remains, and appoint elders in every city as I directed you, namely, if any man be above reproach, the husband of one wife, having children who believe, not accused of dissipation or rebellion. For the overseer must be above reproach as God's steward, not self-willed, not quick-tempered, not addicted to wine, not pugnacious, not fond of sordid gain, but hospitable, loving what is good, sensible, just, devout, self-controlled, holding fast the faithful word which is in accordance with the teaching, that he may be able both to exhort in sound doctrine and to refute those who contradict. [Titus1: 5-9]

Paul is clearly outlining here the process of how to appoint delegated authority in the church to oversee others.   In verses 6-9 below, Paul lists the requirements, the characteristics of those leaders that Titus should appoint to oversee others.

It is a trustworthy statement: if any man aspires to the office of overseer, it is a fine work he desires to do.   An overseer, then, must be above reproach, the husband of one wife, temperate, prudent, respectable, hospitable, able to teach, not addicted to wine or pugnacious, but gentle, uncontentious, free from the love of money.   He must be one who manages his own household well, keeping his children under control with all dignity [but if a man does not know how to manage his own household, how will he take care of the church of God?]; and not a new convert, lest he become conceited and fall into the condemnation incurred by the devil. And he must have a good reputation with those outside the church, so that he may not fall into reproach and the snare of the devil. [1 Timothy 3:1-7]

And from Miletus he sent to Ephesus and called to him the elders of the church.

Be on guard for yourselves and for all the flock, among which the Holy Spirit has made you overseers, to shepherd the church of God which He purchased with His own blood. [Acts 20:17, 28]

God has set up delegated authority in the Church for the building up of the saints.

And He gave some as apostles, and some as prophets, and some as evangelists, and some as pastors and teachers, for the equipping of the saints for the work of service, to the building up of the Body of Christ. [Ephesians 4:11-12]

Do you see it? He has put His delegated authority in the Church for the building up of the body.

Responding to Pastoral Responsibility

The responsibility of a pastor is to disciple the Christians in his church so that they grow to understand who they are in Jesus Christ so they can be a light in the world. It is our challenge to help them understand who they are in Christ so that they can go into the world and make an impact for Jesus Christ.

How should we respond to those individuals God has placed in positions of leadership in the church?

Obey your leaders, and submit to them; for they keep watch over your souls, as those who will give an account. Let them do this with joy and not with grief, for this would be unprofitable for you. [Hebrews 13:17]

Paul is essentially saying, "Listen, if you give them a bunch of grief, if you are always questioning them, always criticizing them, nothing is going to happen in the church. The church will not be profitable for you."

Now I urge you, brethren [you know the household of Stephanas, that they were the first fruits of Achaia, and that they have devoted themselves for ministry to the saints], that you also be in subjection to such men and to everyone who helps in the work and labors.
[1 Corinthians 16:15-16]

Let the elders who rule well be considered worthy of double honor, especially those who work hard at preaching and teaching. [I Timothy 5:17]

REMIND them to be subject to rulers, to authorities, to be obedient, to be ready for every good deed. [Titus 3:1]

It is obvious that God expects His people to submit to His delegated authority in the Church. Now, does that mean that the pastor is better than anyone else? Of course not. Do I think there are people in our church who might do better than I? I wouldn't be surprised! But that is not the point. You may be a better speaker than your pastor, even smarter, but the reality is that your pastor is in the position of authority, not you!

I joke that when the Lord decided he needed another pastor, He looked around, saw me and said, "Hey, Dave, you'll do. Come here." When I received His call to be a pastor my basic response was, "Lord, You've got to be kidding!"

"No, you'll do, Dave. Just trust Me. I'll do the rest."

The governmental flow starts from the pastor, who can then delegate some of his authority to assistant pastors in the church, and to other leadership. But, there is always a governmental flow from God on down. When a person does not submit to the authority in the church, they are rebelling against God. I am not saying the pastor is God, but I am saying that the pastor holds a position of authority in the Body of Christ. And that this authority was given to him by God. When the pastor or other church leadership gives direction, and someone comes against that authority, they are coming against God's delegated authority...and ultimately against God Himself.

Have you noticed that most the arguments in a church are over silly things such as the color of carpet, or the latest hire in the church office? Any change causes problems. I remember one particular Sunday morning when I innocently said, "This platform needs changing. We need to make it more modern." I actually heard people in the congregation gasp! You cannot imagine the concern that one comment caused.

But Dave, My Pastor is Wrong!

Some reading this book might ask, "But Dave, what do I do when our pastor is wrong?" Of course, what that person is really asking most of the time is, "What if I do not agree with my pastor?"

Here is the reality: someone has to lead the church. When you do not agree with the course of the church, sometimes you just need to give the situation to God and let go of it. Maybe you do not like the color of the carpet, but who cares? Stay focused on what God is calling you to do in your church. If you see a problem with a person in leadership, pray for that person and continue to do what God is calling you to do. That is the way the church stays unified and powerful, fully equipped to do some serious damage to the kingdom of darkness.

When you seriously disagree with the leadership of the church you really only have one option: go to that leader and lovingly share your concerns. Your pastor can tell in a millisecond if you are coming from a critical spirit and a critical heart. A true, humble spirit will say, "Pastor, this is how I feel. I am going to share this with you and then it is your problem."

If you have a concern, go to the church leadership, share your concern with them, pray with them, then walk out the door and wash your hands of the situation, continuing to do what God wants you to do.

Submit to the decisions of leadership in the church for the good of the body. Support the leadership. Too many times in the Body of Christ people take offense when their views aren't acted upon. And because they aren't submitted to authority they begin to speak against leadership. Remember, the Bible says, "Out of the mouth speaks that which fills the heart," and too often what fills the heart is rebellion against God's authority.

Over the course of time, whenever the subject of the pastor comes up, a person who has an offense can't help but speak out bad remarks concerning the pastor. And it always amazes me how critical, offended people seem to find each other in the church. Friend, if you are looking for things to complain about, or looking for things that are really wrong with your pastor, I'm sure you can find something.

As a pastor, I am no better than you. There are many people who might be smarter than me, even more spiritual than me. But again, that is not the issue. God placed me in the position of pastor. Since God put me in this position, I know God has put spiritual authority over me. Knowing this, I must be especially careful about what I say to others. My words do have great impact.

There is only one time in the New Testament where we have an example of people refusing to obey delegated authority, and that was in Acts 4 when the Sanhedrin told Peter and the Apostles to stop preaching in the Name of Jesus. The apostles essentially replied, "We must obey God rather than men."

Obviously, if any church leader tells you to do something against the Word of God, or tries to get you into some kind of bondage and control you, you need to say "No thank you" and leave the church. But too often, disagreements in the church come about over nonessential issues that have nothing to do with orthodox Christianity, but only its methods.

If God Led You...Then?

You voluntarily committed yourself to a church. No one put a gun to your head and said, "You must go to that church." If

God led you to the church, then He now expects you to respect the authority in that church.

Trust your pastor.

Since God has instituted His delegated authority in the church, He is also bound by His honor to maintain and defend it. That is a serious reality. I have seen God defend His delegated authority over and over again, dealing quickly with those who oppose His appointed pastors. In fact, I have knelt down and humbly asked God, "Lord, please deal with this person who is causing problems and dissention in the church."

And, I have watched the Lord repeatedly remove the trouble-makers, even sending them out of the city.

Four or five times in our own church we have had people try to sow serious discord. Each time, the dissenter has tried to draw other people to themselves while attacking the credibility of the pastors. As God took those people out of our church to start their own small gathering, I cannot think of one that was blessed.

God does not honor those people who sow discord and dissention, then go off and try and start something new. I've never seen anything good come out of dissention. Usually, within a year or two, the dissenting group is not even meeting anymore. I believe people who instigate dissention pay a precious price because this gossip and dissention is sin and will affect a person's relationship with God until one repents.

Of course, there are many instances where people have left one church to start another, and they have flourished because they made the break in a godly fashion, often with the blessing of the founding church. I would be excited for our church to start another church somewhere under proper leadership and under authority. God blesses that.

Respect Delegated Authority

In 1 Samuel 15, King Saul is rejected by God as being a king of Israel simply because he did not regard Prophet Samuel with the respect he should have. Prophet Samuel came to him and essentially said, "This is what the Lord wants you to do." Saul did not follow the words of the prophet all the way through because King Saul did not regard the prophet's delegated authority. As a result, God took the kingship away from King Saul.

Friend, if you choose to fear God you must respect the delegated authority or find yourself in rebellion against God.

And Moses said, "This will happen when the Lord gives you meat to eat in the evening, and bread to the full in the morning; for the Lord hears your grumblings which you grumble against Him. And what are we? Your grumblings are not against us but against the Lord."
[Exodus 16:8]

Moses responded to the grumblings and complaining against him because they did not have water. Moses talked to God and got the Israelites water. Next, they became angry because they did not have meat and bread to eat. Again, they grumbled at Moses who essentially said, "Hey, I didn't want this job. I was happy in Midian until I experienced this burning bush. So here I am. Don't you understand that you are not grumbling against me and Aaron? You are grumbling against the Lord."

Even as a pastor, whenever or wherever I come in contact with God's delegated authority in another ministry, I try to be consistently careful about what I say about her or him. In these last few years in our Christian culture, we have seen so many self-appointed judges who have persecuted, maligned, slandered, and gossiped against their fellow Christian brothers and sisters. Most of these persecutions and accusations are usually about non-essential issues or about methodology.

People castigate leaders in the Body of Christ over such nonsense, and they are in trouble with God. Let me give you an example.

In the 70s and 80s there was a particular individual on the radio who was one of the most-listened-to Christian talk show hosts in California. He owned hundreds of radio stations. During that time, there was "the Charismatic renewal" when God's Holy Spirit awoke in the Church, renewing the truth about the importance of the baptism of the Holy Spirit [and speaking in tongues]. This movement shot across all denominational lines. Presbyterians, Lutherans, Catholics, etc. were all coming into this new fullness of the Holy Spirit. However, this man was rabidly against the movement! He would come on the radio every day and rile against these leaders and against the speaking in tongues [which he maintained was of the devil]. In the 80s he wrote a book called *88 Reasons Why Jesus Christ is Coming in September of 1988.* When I first saw that book, I thought, "Oh boy, here it comes. God's judgment is coming on this guy!"

Many people in my church showed me this book and quoted from it, giving "biblical reasons" why the end was going to happen in September, 1988. The book sold thousands of copies. Of course, September of 1988 came and went and Jesus did not come back. This man became totally discredited in most of the Body of Christ.

This is what I believed happened.

God let a deluding spirit influence this man because of his pride and rebellion against God's anointed authority in the Church. This man is still on the radio, but his opinions have become very fringe. Few take him seriously. He is now preaching that all Christians should leave their churches, that the Church is not God's way of reaching this generation!

I believe this example shows that when you touch God's anointed in a negative way, you touch God in a negative way, as well.

Youth Pastor and Critic

Let me share one personal experience about how the area of spiritual authority really hit home for me.

After I graduated from seminary I had a Masters of Divinity degree and I knew I was ready to go! I had given up my secular "career," had exhausted all my funds, and was living at my aunt's house, waiting for God to use me. I told God, "Let's go! Your man of faith and power is ready!"

Well, it was like God forgot about me. But eventually, He did lead me to be a youth pastor of a church.

The pastor of that church did most things totally different than I would have. Now, please understand that my feelings had nothing to do with his love for Jesus, or his commitment to the Lord, or his wanting to see people grow in Christ and be saved. It had to do with his methodology, how he dealt with the youth and the congregation! Everything he did was absolutely the opposite of how I would have done it.

Ultimately and unfortunately, I arrived at the point where I really believed that this man was the biggest hindrance to God's Holy Spirit working among the people in that church. I actually blamed him for God not moving there. I filled myself with a critical spirit, and soon I was talking to everyone in the church, sowing seeds of dissention. I was headed for destruction, but in God's wisdom and grace He placed into my hands a book called *Spiritual Authority* by Watchman Nee.

As I read the book, the truth about what I had been doing hit me like a 2" x 4" across the head! My eyes were opened and I understood that I was in trouble by coming against God's authority, and ultimately, against God. As I read the book, I had an experience with God and totally repented, deciding to be the best youth pastor this church and that pastor had ever experienced. I determined that whatever vision the pastor had, I would come out 100% for that vision, supporting both the vision and the pastor. Nothing negative was going to come out of my mouth ever again!

Now, here is the incredible miracle about this revelation.

I had been vainly trying to start a church for two years, with many false starts, which was very discouraging. But within two months after making that decision to honor and support the pastor, God shot me out of a cannon and a group of people said to me, "Dave, we want you to be our pastor." Shortly thereafter,

I was standing in front of a group of people on a Sunday morning preaching the Word of God as their pastor.

That was not an accident!

God could not release me to more responsibility until I learned the importance of submitting to delegated authority.

Paul's Pride and the Fall

It seems obvious from Scripture that Paul was probably a prideful guy before his conversion.

Paul was on an important job, on his way to Damascus, with a letter signed personally by the High Priest, the highest political office in Judaism [both a political and a religious office] [Acts 9]. So, Mr. High-and-Mighty Saul was going to Damascus when God took him off his high horse. God blinded this Pharisee of Pharisees who knew the Pentateuch and the Old Testament prophets backwards and forwards. Paul as a Pharisee had most likely memorized the first five books of the Old Testament: Genesis, Exodus, Leviticus, Numbers, and Deuteronomy.

After dealing with the blinded Paul for three days, God sent to him little-known Ananias, a godly man, but with little training compared to Paul. Paul had to humble himself, submit to God's delegated authority, and receive from this untrained man from Damascus. But he understood that Ananias was the man at that particular time that God was using as His instrument for Paul's life. That is an excellent picture of how you and I should react to the delegated authority God places in our lives.

Don't Grumble Against God's Anointed

Are you willing to submit to God's delegated authority in your life and in your church?

Young people, your primary authority is your parents! Do not tell me that you love God but you are not willing to obey your parents! If you want to submit yourself to God, God is giving your parents authority in your life right now.

Wives, submit to your husbands, not because they are better than you, but because God has given them the spiritual authority in the household.

Men, totally submit yourself to God's Word and to the spiritual authorities God has placed over you. When another brother comes to you and opens the Word of God, telling you that you are really blowing it in a particular area, remember at that moment that person is God's delegated authority in your life because he is coming to you with the Word.

Remember, rebelling against God's delegated authority has its consequences. When someone like Ananias comes to you and says, "You know, I see what you are doing. But this is what the Word of God says," at that moment he is God's delegated authority over your life because he is speaking for God. How you react to that instruction exposes whether or not you are submitted to the Lord Jesus Christ.

In Numbers 16 we see that 250 leaders in Israel are coming up against Moses.

And they assembled together against Moses and Aaron, and said to them, "You have gone far enough, for all the congregation are holy, every one of them, and the LORD is in their midst; so why do you exalt yourselves above the assembly of the LORD?" [Numbers 16:3]

God caused the earth to open up and swallow all 250 of the critical leaders, along with their wives and kids. The next day the ignorant Israelites started to grumble against Moses again, complaining that he had killed their leaders. Now if I had been there and heard that grumbling, I hope I would have said, "Mary, go get the kids. We are going to get away from here now, as fast as we can, because something bad is coming."

And, I would have been right. Because of the grumbling, God released a plague against them the next day!

Moses was an incredible person. I probably would have said, "God, go get the grumblers. Strike them dead!" Instead, Moses knelt down and interceded for the plague to stop.

It did, but only after 14,700 Israelites died.

In Numbers 12, Aaron and Miriam are very critical of Moses because after his wife died he took another wife. They did not approve of the woman he selected. Well, God called Aaron and Miriam out and essentially said, "Who do you think you are?" Miriam ended up with leprosy.

Leviticus 10 tells us about men who subverted Aaron's priesthood and authority. God's fire from heaven consumed them.

Are you seeing a pattern?

David Understood Authority

King David understood spiritual authority better than most in the Bible. The Lord called David a man "after My own heart." David respected authority when he knew that authority came from God.

In 1 Samuel 24, Saul was chasing David with 3000 of his choicest men. They intended to kill him. Samuel had already anointed David as king, so David and his followers knew it was only a matter of time.

Yet, at the moment, David and his men were hiding in a cave to escape Saul and his 3000 men. Here, God was testing David. At the cave, Saul goes in to relieve himself, not knowing David and his men are in the cave. At that moment, Saul is in a very vulnerable position. David's men encouraged him to "kill him and you'll be king." David refused, essentially saying, "Far be it for me to do this thing against the Lord's anointed." David persuaded his men not to rise up against Saul.

In 1 Samuel 26, David could have killed Saul, but instead decided to allow God to deal with Saul. David refused to take matters into his own hands, rather waiting and trusting on God to deal with His delegated authority.

We all need to be careful concerning our attitudes, thoughts, words and deeds against God's delegated authority. We must not undermine spiritual leadership in any way because we might hinder what God is trying to do through the Body of Christ, and in our lives.

When you come across a person sowing discord and dissention in the church, questioning, criticizing and demeaning leadership, here's what the Bible tells you to do:

Now I urge you, brethren, keep your eye on those who cause dissensions and hindrances contrary to the teaching, which you learned, and turn away from them. For such men are slaves, not of our Lord Christ but of their own appetites; and by their smooth and flattering speech they deceive the hearts of the unsuspecting.

[Romans 16:17-18]

Pride is frequently the source of the dissention, and for some reason, proud people try to gather as many other people as they can to join in their dissention. Paul tells us to "turn away" from them.

Remember, if we fear God we will submit to His authority in the church.

CHAPTER NINE

Fearing God in Your Marriage?

If you have made a decision to fear God with your life, what implication does that have on how you live in your marriage?

As a single person, how does fearing God impact the type of person you may select to marry?

If you are single and reading this book, you might be thinking, "Great, an entire chapter on marriage. I'm going to skip this chapter." If that's you, please stay with me. It is important for you, even as a single person, to understand the basic foundational truths concerning the roles and responsibilities of the husband and wife. Even if you plan on *never* getting married, you will always have married friends who need to know what the Bible says.

Now on the last day, the great day of the feast, Jesus stood and cried out, saying, "If any man is thirsty, let him come to Me and drink. He who believes in Me, as the Scripture said, 'From his innermost being shall flow rivers of living water.'" [John 7:37-38]

Jesus said to them,

"I am the bread of life; he who comes to Me shall not hunger, and he who believes in Me shall never thirst."
[John 6:35]

These two scriptures are foundational to having a good marriage. They reveal that Jesus has the spiritual food prepared to satisfy our innermost desires and needs, including in the area of marriage. Jesus is essentially saying through these scriptures:

"Do you want to have a good marriage? Do you want to have your needs met in your marriage as I have ordained? Do you want to be able to tell everyone what a wonderful marriage you have, what a wonderful spouse you have, how blessed you are? Then come to Me. Do things My way, take seriously what I have to say and your innermost needs will be satisfied!"

Jesus is inviting us to look to Him and experience marriage as He meant it to be! Marriage God's way.

Hope for Every Troubled Marriage

There is hope for every marriage, no matter how bad it might appear currently. Any couple who seriously seeks God and asks Him for answers can change!

AND, your marriage can be transformed regardless of what your spouse does! The road to a good marriage starts with you, not your spouse.

Ultimately, you are only responsible for yourself. You cannot be held accountable if your spouse decides not to obey God. No matter how your spouse responds, the Bible promises that if you trust, believe, and hope in God with your life, you will not be disappointed! You will be blessed.

As you read this chapter, make a decision to be part of the solution, not the problem.

A Solid Marriage Foundation

Therefore everyone who hears these words of Mine, and acts upon them, may be compared to a wise man, who built his house upon the rock. And the rain descended, and the floods came, and the winds blew, and burst against that house; and yet it did not fall, for it had been founded upon the rock. And everyone who hears these words of Mine, and does not act upon them, will be like a foolish man, who built his house upon the sand. And the rain descended, and the floods came, and the winds blew, and burst against that house; and it fell, and great was its fall. The result was that when Jesus had finished these words, the multitudes were amazed at His teaching; for He was teaching them as one having authority, and not as their scribes. [Matthew 7:24-29]

The truth here is really quite simple: If you reject God's plans for marriage, you are going to suffer the consequences, especially when troubles come into your life. If your marriage is not based on a firm biblical foundation concerning what God says about roles and responsibilities of both the man and the woman, when troubles come, your marriage is going to experience some very serious problems.

On the other hand, if you build your marriage on the biblical principles God has set forth, when troubles come not only will you weather the marriage storm, but you will emerge victorious.

My wife, Mary, and I had some serious problems early on in our marriage. One day I realized that I was trying to make Mary think like me. When she didn't, I became very upset. Of course, she too was having the same problem. After awhile I began to realize that my wife was never going to think like me...and that's a *good* thing! Our diverse thinking brings balance into our marriage.

To fear God is to make a choice, to do things God's way, to submit to His biblical principles. God will bless anyone who takes His Word seriously in marriage.

There's Always Hope

There's hope for your marriage, no matter what state it is in now. Do not let your emotions, your anger, your pride, other people, a book or a family member convince you otherwise!

Your hope starts with surrendering, then yielding your marriage to Jesus. When you hope in Him, you will never be disappointed! The road to transforming your marriage starts with you saying, "God, what do You want me to do? What are my roles and responsibilities in this marriage? I submit to you."

God's Stand on Divorce

God does not want you divorced.

"For I hate divorce," says the Lord, the God of Israel, "and him who covers his garment with wrong," says the Lord of hosts. "So take heed to your spirit, that you do not deal treacherously." [Malachi 2:16]

Obviously, God feels very strongly about divorce. The next question is, "Do you feel strongly about it?"

As divorce has increased in our society, the Church has been reluctant to take a firm stand against it for fear it would hurt church growth. As divorces increased, the Church focus shifted to love, forgiveness, and grace. Now, I'm glad for these three gifts, but when it comes to divorce, the Church message should be: "Divorce is our enemy. There are consequences to a divorce. Don't do it!"

If you are a divorced person reading this, do not let the enemy try and put you in some kind of condemnation, especially if you are now remarried. Focus on the marriage you are in, to make it the best it can be.

I am absolutely convinced that generally divorce is wrong. When divorce does happen, even with biblical justification, it still should be the very last resort, after prayer and counseling. Many differ on what constitutes a biblical right for divorce. Personally, I believe that theologically there are three reasons: adultery [Matt. 9:9], desertion [1 Cor. 7:15], and if they killed you for it in the Old Testament. [If they killed you, there wasn't any need for divorce.] [i.e., homosexuality, sorcery, etc.] If you had a divorce for unbiblical reasons, I hope you have repented and have asked the Lord to forgive you for rejecting His Word. Then, tell Him that you are committed to His Word in your current covenant relationship. You may have been divorced four times, but if you *really* repent and seek after God now, He'll bless your current marriage. Jesus is only concerned about the marriage you have right now!

After decades of experience, it is clear that divorce is bad. Divorce destroys. The consequences of divorce are far-reaching for both adults and children. Some say, "It is better to get a divorce than to have the kids live with the bickering and fighting." Evidence shows that the children receive the most severe consequences from a divorce. Divorce makes a child four times as likely to commit a violent crime, and increases his chances of dropping out of school, of abusing alcohol and drugs, of becoming sexually promiscuous. If you have children, the greatest gift you can give them is to stay together.

Divorce impacts even newly married couples, filling many of them with insecurity and fear. Every time there is an argument they wonder, "Where is this going to lead? Are we going to stay together?"

Divorce must be our enemy. Learn to hate it the way God hates it.

"I Don't Believe That! God's wrong."

Most troubled marriages are usually the result of a spouse's disobedience to the foundational truths of the roles and responsibilities that God has placed for them in the Bible.

> *Unless the Lord builds the house, they labor in vain who build it; unless the Lord guards the city, the watchman keeps awake in vain. [Psalm 127:1]*

What are you building your marriage on? If you are a Christian, there can be only one foundation...Jesus Christ and the Word of God.

In Ephesians 5, the Apostle Paul gives us three foundational truths concerning marriage, and the foundational roles and responsibilities as husbands and wives. When I read this scripture to married couples who are having trouble, not once in twenty years have I had them disagree with this passage. I've never had one person say, "I don't believe that! God's wrong!"

Instead, I hear them say, "I can't do that" because they are afraid their spouse is going to take advantage of them. "If I really do that, my spouse will run all over me. I can't trust her response. It would be a nightmare."

The road to a successful marriage starts with you, and the road to turning around a troubled marriage starts with you obeying and trusting the Word of God! I have witnessed many miraculous marriage turnarounds when spouses humble themselves and submit to God.

One woman I know had been domineering and controlling in her marriage for over 25 years, then she got saved. This woman started to take seriously her roles and responsibilities in marriage, especially where the Lord said to submit to her husband's leadership. After about three months, her husband woke her at 2:00 a.m. and said, "I can't stand this anymore! What has happened to you? Suddenly you are everything I have ever wanted. What has changed you? It is the church you're going to?"

She opened up the Word of God and explained to him her role in marriage. The man's mouth dropped open, and he said, "If God can do that for you, I want Him in my life right now." He then knelt down and received Jesus.

Do not ever underestimate the power of obeying the Word of God in your marriage!

In the same way, you wives, be submissive to your own husbands so that even if any of them are disobedient to the word, they may be won without a word by the behavior of their wives. [1 Peter 3:1]

Three Foundational Truths

In almost every Bible translation, the word "submit" best communicates what God is talking about here, so I am going to use that word in my writing.

Wives, be subject [submissive] to your own husbands, as to the Lord. For the husband is the head of the wife, as Christ also is the head of the church, He Himself being the Savior of the body. But as the church is subject [submissive] to Christ, so also the wives ought to be to their husbands in everything. Husbands, love your wives, just as Christ also loved the church and gave Himself up for her; that He might sanctify her, having cleansed her by the washing of water with the word, that He might present to Himself the church in all her glory, having no spot or wrinkle or any such thing; but that she should be holy and blameless. So husbands ought also to love their own wives as their own bodies. He who loves his own wife loves himself; for no one ever hated his own flesh, but nourish and cherish it, just as Christ also does the church, because we are members of His body. FOR THIS CAUSE A MAN SHALL LEAVE HIS FATHER AND MOTHER, AND SHALL CLEAVE TO HIS WIFE; AND THE TWO SHALL BECOME ONE FLESH. This mystery is great; but I am speaking with reference to Christ and the church. Nevertheless let each individual among you also love his own wife even as himself; and let the wife see to it that she respect her husband. [Ephesians 5:22-33]

These verses reveal three foundational truths concerning marriage.

Foundation Truth # 1:
Marriage is a covenant.

In verses 23, 24, 25, 27, 29, 30, 32a, comparison is being made between God's covenant with the Church and the covenant between a husband and wife.

What is a covenant? It is an agreement where two parties vow to keep commitments and practices with one another. The Bible is filled with such covenants.

God made covenants with Abraham, Moses, Isaac, Noah, David, and the Levites. God gave them "conditional covenants," meaning He essentially said, "If you do this, I will respond in this manner. If you obey My commands, I will bless you."

Deuteronomy 28 is loaded with conditional covenant promises. One example is Deuteronomy 7:9:

Know therefore that the LORD your God, He is God, the faithful God, who keeps His covenant and His loving kindness to a thousandth generation with those who love Him and keep His commandments.

As we read through the Bible it is easy to discern that God judges His people by how they keep His covenant with them. In the New Testament, we have a new covenant with God that is based on the death and resurrection of Jesus Christ.

Jesus said:

I am the resurrection and the life; he who believes in Me shall live even if he dies, and everyone who lives and believes in Me shall never die. Do you believe this?
[John 11: 25-26]

When you receive Jesus Christ as your Lord and Savior, He gives you eternal life, starting right now! There are two aspects to your eternal life: <u>One</u>: When the body dies, your spirit and soul live on forever, and <u>Two</u>: You have eternal life starting when you accept Jesus. He declared that in this eternal life there is abundance, a way to live that can bless you in your life, your marriage, your finances. [John 10:10] Just look to Him first and submit to His Word, and you will be blessed.

The Bible is an invitation to study God's faithfulness in keeping His covenant. The longer I live as a Christian, the more I can testify that God is a covenant-keeping God. God keeps His promises.

On our wedding day Mary and I made a covenant to be faithful to each other. That covenant is a reflection of the Church. God always remains faithful to us, and so too Mary and I are to always remain faithful to each other. God invites anyone who would want to put Him to the test to see that He keeps covenant with the Church. Christian couples in the Church cannot separate character and integrity from their faithfulness in keeping covenant. If we do not keep covenant, we do not have integrity and character

We are called to be covenant keepers. Our word should be our bond. Our testimony to the world outside the Church is that if we make a promise, we keep our covenants.

When I married my wife it was for life, through the good times and through the problems. I'll never forget one day my wife looked at me with fire in her eyes and declared, "I hate you." I thought to myself, "This woman has some major problems!" I called a marriage counselor and explained, "My wife has major problems. Her emotional responses are being dictated by her past hurts and dysfunctions. Mary needs some major healing and I feel you and your wife are the perfect counselors for her."

Of course, it did not take long for me to figure out that I was one of the major problems in our marriage. In the midst of our challenge, <u>divorce did not come up</u>! It was never an option. Even though Mary did not want to be around me, she knew that divorce was not an option. We had two choices: 1] We could continue to be miserable, or 2] We could decide to take steps such as counseling to fix it. We decided to work on improving our marriage.

Neither Mary nor I could walk away from the covenant we made with each other and God. To do that, we would have had to turn our backs on God.

Foundation Truth # 2:
Wives are to submit to their husbands.

The following verses all speak of a woman submitting to her husband. This is not a debatable biblical truth. Ladies, submitting to your husband has nothing to do with your husband being superior. It has to do with him being appointed by God as the designated head of the marriage union.

Wives, be subject to your own husbands, as to the Lord. For the husband is the head of the wife, as Christ also is the head of the church, He Himself being the Savior of the body. But as the church is subject to Christ, so also the wives ought to be to their husbands in everything.
[Ephesians 5:22-24]

In the same way, you wives, be submissive to your own husbands so that even if any of them are disobedient to the word, they may be won without a word by the behavior of their wives. [1 Peter 3:1]

To be sensible, pure, workers at home, kind, being subject to their own husbands, that the word of God may not be dishonored. [Titus 2:5]

Let a woman quietly receive instruction with entire submissiveness. [1 Timothy 2:11-13]

The Bible is very clear: there is no partiality with God. In the Kingdom of God there is no Greek, no Hebrew, no male or female...there are just His children, and He loves them all equally. The area of submission has nothing to do with a woman as an individual, it has to do with the order of God's authority.

Wives are called to submit to the spiritual authority God has placed upon their husbands. God is not calling you to submit to a man but to the spiritual authority God has placed on him. In the military, when a uniformed sergeant and uniformed captain meet, the sergeant salutes the captain because of his authority. When the sergeant sees the captain at a ballgame where both are out of uniform, he does not salute because the Constitution says we are "created equal." The authority of that captain rests in the office when he is in uniform, under the authority of the military.

In the military, one man or one woman is not better. It is respect for the authority that governs...respect for the uniform. Ladies, when you submit to your husband, you are submitting to God's authority on your husband. Ultimately, you are submitting yourself to the Lord.

A woman in submission is submitting to God's divine authority. God's submission is basically an attitude of one's heart. It is the overall way a woman responds to her husband. Submission does not mean a wife loses her individuality and becomes a doormat, submitting to abuse or sin. She can be submissive to his authority and still say, "No, I won't do that. It is inconsistent with the Word of God." Or, "Dear, could we seek some counsel before I do what you ask because I'm afraid it is in conflict with God's Word."

That is a godly attitude of the heart.

A wife can be submitted and still disagree, holding her own opinions.

Submission simply involves honoring the authority God has placed upon your husband. Honoring your husband is ultimately trusting God. God is going to bless you as you honor and submit to the authority He has placed on your husband. Do not fret about what your husband decides to do with that authority. You are ONLY responsible for your own actions. Your husband is in God's hands.

After over twenty years of being a pastor, I'm convinced that a man craves honor in the marriage even more than sex. A man needs to feel that when he comes home he is honored and respected as the leader of the home.

A quick note to single ladies: Do not marry a man if you are not willing to submit to him because that submission is foundational to the success of your marriage. If you feel you cannot submit to the man you are planning to marry, then do not marry him! You will not change the man, only God can do that. Your nurturing is not going to change him. Until you can honestly say, "Yes, I can submit to him," postpone the marriage and get some counseling.

Foundation Truth # 3:
The husband is the servant-leader.

Paul has more to say to the husband than he does the wife because the husband is the designated leader in the marriage. So, the husband ultimately is going to take on the most responsibility if that marriage fails. If you own a business, and that business fails, the person in leadership—the owner—will receive most of the blame for the failure.

Whether we like it or not, God expects men to be servant-leaders in the home. For 200 years our country experienced relative calm and stability in our society, I believe, because men understood their responsibilities in the home, in the community, and in their church. In these last three decades we have seen that leadership fail. Satan has done a very good job in breaking down the family and launching an attack on manhood. Satan understands that if he can belittle and make irrelevant a man's leadership, especially in the family, he will destroy society.

Many men who have fallen away from God have rejected God's role in their lives to be leaders, abdicating their responsibility. The result is a generation of angry kids. Our church works extensively with young people, and we know there are many angry kids, without the leadership of a father, who do not even know why they are angry. When you look into their histories, almost all of these angry children have dads who have abdicated their responsibilities.

The director of a prison ministry tells me this shocking story.

A man in prison who was a very good artist came to the Lord. The chaplain thought that since Father's Day was coming up, he would challenge his new artist convert to design a Father's Day card which could be sold to raise some money for the chapel. Out of 1,280 prisoners, not one person bought a card! After this rather sobering experience, the prison chaplain began to investigate the backgrounds of the 1,280 inmates, and could not find even one who had any kind of decent relationship with his father!

Men, do not ever think you are unimportant to your children!

If you know a young person, or are related to a young person who has no relationship with their father, pray for those kids. If your wife has taken away your children and you cannot see them on a regular basis, you can pray for them on a regular basis. Pray and believe God that a time will come when you will be able to be a father to your children.

Pray something like, "God protect my child who is angry and doesn't even know why. Please protect him until I can come into his/her life once again and we can work through this thing. Lord, move Your Spirit to heal their broken heart."

As husbands, we are to follow the example of Jesus and love our wives as Christ loved the Church. We see how He loved in Matthew 20:28.

The Son of Man did not come to be served, but to serve, and to give His life a ransom for many.

We are to give our lives to our wives first, and then to our children. That means denying one's self for the good of your wife and family. A godly husband surrenders his agendas, his hobbies, his needs to serve his wife and family. I freely admit I had the wrong attitude when I entered into marriage with Mary. In my mind, she was there for me! When you look at the problems we have had in our marriage, most of them stemmed from my "me first" attitude. When I finally understood that I was to minister to her needs first, then our marriage changed radically!

Husbands, when there is a choice between what you want to do [fishing, golfing, watching the tube] or serving your wife and your kids, serve your wife and kids...that's being a servant leader. Some may say, "Then what about my needs?" Sir, if you want your needs met abundantly, beyond what you can ask or think...*serve your wife.* When I put my wife first, I'm blessed.

Once my wife told me that when I help her with the dishes, or when she sees me reading to the kids, she falls in love with me all over again. Men, take it from me...nothing will cause your wife to love you and meet your needs more than if she knows you are sacrificially giving of yourself to her and the children as the servant-leader.

The 555 Marriage Plan

In our church I have introduced what I call the 555 Marriage Plan, a proven plan to enhance your marriage. In this plan, the husband and wife agree to do the following:

1. Pray together for 5 minutes each day.

The husband starts by praying God's blessing on his wife, and then the wife prays a blessing on her husband. I tell the married couples in our church, "If you are a Christian couple and cannot agree to pray together for five minutes each day, you have some serious marriage problems."

Something very important here: Wives, if your husband forgets to pray on a particular day with you, do not fall into ungodly thoughts such as, "There's proof that he doesn't care about our marriage." The enemy will try and lead you into ungodly thoughts, so resist the devil and he must flee. Instead, pray for your husband, give him grace. Let the Holy Spirit convict him that he missed a day.

2.   Read God's Word together 5 minutes each day.

You can start at the beginning of God's Word and go methodically through it, or you can pick a favorite book of the Bible and read there. It is important only that God's Word saturate your spirit every day.

I can guarantee that if you pray for 5 minutes each day and read your Bible for 5 minutes each day, your marriage will greatly improve, even if it is a great marriage now.

3.   Read and Pray 5 times a week.

I suggest 5 days a week because couples are extremely busy, and sometimes you are going to miss. When you do, you still have Saturday and Sunday to make up for any day you may have missed during the week.

It is so easy to become distracted from the things of God. When Mary and I were coordinating the sub-contractors who were building our home, we did not pray or read the Bible together like we should. As one who has fallen into the "too busy" trap, I urge you to not allow anything to distract you from the 555 Marriage Plan!

If you follow this plan faithfully, I can guarantee that your marriage will flourish and prosper. It does really come down to this basic truth. Fear the Lord in your marriage and you will be blessed.

CHAPTER TEN

The Responsibilities of a Father Who Fears the Lord

Behold, I will send you Elijah the prophet before the coming of the great and dreadful day of the LORD: And he shall turn the heart of the fathers to the children, and the heart of the children to their fathers, lest I come and smite the earth with a curse. [Malachi 4:5-6]

Malachi 4:5-6 talks about a curse coming upon a whole nation when the fathers' hearts are not turned toward their children. Today, we have an entire generation of hurting children, angry kids, who do not have the maturity to process their anger. Much of that anger comes from the fact that so many do not have a real relationship with their father, or their father has abdicated his roles and responsibilities.

I once heard a man on a Christian radio station who headed an organization trying to promote fatherhood in the United States. His contention was that kids without fathers were frequently violent, committed rapes, and even murdered because they do not know how to process their anger.

Fatherless, they become destructive and rebellious.

My father, a lifetime pastor, told me over thirty years ago, when we were riding in a car, that there is "...a pacifying of the American male, especially married men. They are abdicating their responsibilities. I am really concerned about what this means for the future of our country."

Many American men have given up their leadership roles as the father in the family, letting others make decisions for them: psychologists, teachers, principals, and even the children

165

themselves, because it is easier to let someone else do it. Too often in America the father's heart is not toward their children, but somewhere else, be it in sports, fishing, golf, T.V., etc.

We have an entire generation of angry, hurting kids whose fathers have abdicated their responsibilities, so their angry children rebel. Men need to be liberated from the curse of abandoning God's ordained roles for their lives.

Women need to be liberated too—from bad male leadership. I pray that there is a rising determination in men from the Holy Spirit that is saying something along these lines: "I want to be different. I want to do it God's way, I want to be blessed. I want my marriage to be blessed, I want my children to be blessed."

If you are a single man, I hope you are looking to the future and are saying, "I am going to do it God's way. If I ever get married I want to embrace God's roles and responsibilities for me in marriage."

A man's man is God's man.

There is nothing men can do that will change this society more than to become men who take on the responsibility God has called them to assume in their families.

Roles and Responsibilities of a Father

One of the important scriptures in my life is Proverbs 13:22.

A good man leaves an inheritance for his children's children.

I believe that I am supposed to leave a financial inheritance for my children. If I teach them to be good stewards, they are going to leave a financial inheritance to their children, who can then pass it on to their children. The Kingdom of God will be enriched because there will be ample money to do the works of the Kingdom.

I also believe that I need to leave a *spiritual and emotional inheritance* to my children. I need to leave a legacy of living a biblical life to my children.

166

I want to leave a legacy so that my children's children are a positive influence to their society, living according to the Word of God.

I do not just want to influence my three kids, I want to influence three or four generations down the line! I believe I have a responsibility to think about these things. I love my children's children and I do not even know who they are yet! I want them to love Jesus, to be a blessing to their culture.

I am convinced that being a godly father can be condensed down to two main scriptures.

Main Scripture # 1: Ephesians 6:4

Fathers, do not provoke your children to anger but bring them up in the discipline and instruction of the Lord.

When you do not take seriously the roles and responsibilities as a father, your children are going to become angry. Because they do not know how to process that anger, they will become rebellious and destructive, frequently self destructive.

Main Scripture # 2: Colossians 3:21

Fathers, do not exasperate your children that they may not lose heart.

These two verses explain why kids rebel, and do destructive things to themselves and society. When the father treats the mother poorly, when the father abdicates his responsibility to provide for the family and abandons his children, or when he criticizes them constantly, when he withholds love from them, when he does not discipline them, when he does not give up his time for them, when he does not set an example for his children, they become angry and exasperated, they lose heart, they become destructive and rebellious.

Servant Leadership

My role as a father is to be a **servant-leader**. I lead by serving my wife and my children and fulfilling my responsibilities as a father.

As a pastor, I meet many people, and am privy to many events that happen in people's families. In many ways, I am like a scientist who sees this human experiment of marriage being played out before my very eyes. As a result, I have learned some valuable things that I have embraced with my own children.

Start to declare right now that "I am going to leave my children a legacy. Yes, I know I have done some things I shouldn't have done, but I am starting right now to live for Jesus. Lord, I will do what You want me to do whenever You give me an opportunity. Lord, I want to consistently plant seeds of truth in my kids' lives and start praying for them. I want to be the kind of Dad you called me to be."

Six Responsibilities of a Father

For the balance of this chapter, I want to share the six basic responsibilities of a father to his children.

Responsibility # 1:   Lead by example

Men lead by following the example of Jesus Christ.
Men lead in the home by serving.

Jesus did not come to be served but to serve and give his life as a ransom for many. [Matthew 20:28]

The greater your spiritual responsibility, the more you should strive to be a servant! You cannot be a leader in the Kingdom of God without being a servant! As a father, when there is a choice between going golfing, watching television, taking a nap, or whatever else you want to do, and being with your children, or addressing a family situation, or being with your wife...it is always them and never you.

Leading by example means you deny yourself.

You may be asking, "Dave, what about me? What about my needs?"

Luke 6:38 says, "Give and it shall be given unto you." If you want your needs met as a father, husband, man, and human, serve your family and I will guarantee that, if you have a godly wife, the needs that you have will be met abundantly, beyond what you ask and think!

When our kids sense that we would give our lives for them, that we would never lie to them, that we always want to do the best for them, they begin to trust us. When your children grow older, you can lead them the way you want to because they trust you. They will say to themselves, "I know that Dad has the best in mind for me. He loves me, and would do anything for me. I've seen it all my life. I've seen his integrity, his commitment to the Lord Jesus and to my mother. I've witnessed his willingness to forgive, and his honest, hard work. I can see the blessings in his life. I'm going to follow my father as he follows Christ."

Your children will embrace your value system because it is God's value system and it produces an abundant life. If you live God's value system in your life, if you take those rules and responsibilities seriously, it is going to impact your children for the good, and your kids will have no reason to rebel. Of course, all children will eventually try to stretch their wings a bit, but as you lead, they will eventually follow.

As a pastor I have the benefit of watching people raise their children using different methods. Without exception, the strong families have dads who are leaders in the home, and who have been examples to their children. These fathers have not given their children any reason to rebel.

When the Bible says, *"Train up a child in the way that he should go and when he/she grows old they will not depart from it,"* it is not just talking about information! There's an old saying, "More is caught than taught." Train your children by making sure they attend church, go to Bible studies, and care about their education but also make sure they see you living out your faith on a daily basis.

If you want rebellious kids, live a hypocritical life and you will be in for a long hard ride. How you live your life teaches your kids more than any information you could give them.

Responsibility # 2:   Set the Standards.

Set the biblical standard as to what is acceptable and not acceptable in the house. Belief in God's Word should be the basis of our lives. Even if you fail, or let your wife down, or disobey God, your family knows you will go to God and ask Him to forgive you.

I want my kids to know, "We are the Hoffmans, and we live by the Word of God. We keep our promises. We do not lie or cheat. We are the Hoffmans, we respect authority, are loyal to our friends, and have compassion on those who are less fortunate then we are. The Hoffmans live by biblical standards. We go to church every Sunday because we want to hear the Word of God for our lives, and honor God on a regular basis, putting him first. We read our Bible and pray because we want God's Spirit, power and truth to permeate our lives. We're active in our church because God has given us a ministry of reconciliation. We're going to be a part of transforming our community."

My children know that we live by biblical standards.

Fathers, we have the primary responsibility to teach our kids the Word of God.

I have made a covenant with the Lord Jesus to sit down consistently with my kids and either read the Bible to them or have them read it to me, and then talk about what we've read.

Fathers, God has called us to set the standard.

Responsibility # 3:   Discipline your children.

It is our responsibility to make sure our children are consistently and fairly disciplined because our kids [like their Dads] are sinners. They have a sin nature, and are not naturally good. But, if you raise them up in a good environment, and parent them correctly, giving them self esteem, building them up, as they grow older they will make right choices.

But left to themselves, they are not holy little angels.

The heart is more deceitful than all else, it is desperately sick. [Jeremiah 17:9]

Proverbs 22:15 says this,

Foolishness is bound up in the heart of a child.

Many educators maintain that man is basically good, but scripture indicates otherwise! We are all born with a sinful nature. But, the rod of discipline will remove the foolishness out of your child.

The Apostle Paul put it this way in Romans 7:18:

I know that nothing good lives in me, that is, in my sinful nature.

God lives in our spirit, and there is always a war going on between our flesh [our sinful nature] and our spirit. But, God has given us His power to walk in the spirit and not in the flesh.

Fathers, we need to teach our kids that there are consequences for their behavior, so they need to learn to make their choices based on biblical standards so the only consequences are blessings instead of curses.

Discipline your children now, so that when they become teenagers they will make biblical decisions instead of decisions based on feelings, emotions, and whims. Teach them that when they disobey the Word of God, when they disobey authority, there are consequences.

America has an entire generation of young people who have never learned the reality of facing consequences for their behavior. As a result, they have no self-control because nobody has disciplined them. When I was in school, and you did something wrong, they marched you down to the principal's office to receive physical discipline, and then wait for your parents to show up. I received discipline twice, once from the school, and then from my parents! And, my parents never listened to my excuses—the school was right, I was wrong.

Period. "They are your authority," they would tell me, "and you must respect them."

Today, parents go to the school to fight with the administration. I personally know many teachers who are extremely frustrated because when a discipline problem comes up, the parents come to the school angry, ready to blame the school for the problem.

Parents do not want the responsibility to discipline!

Fathers have the primary responsibility for discipline, and the Mother also has some responsibility in this area. To reinforce her discipline responsibilities, I tell my kids on a regular basis that "If you mess with mother you mess with me." Mary knows she can always call me to come home and reinforce her discipline, and the kids know that is not a good thing [thankfully, that happens very seldom]!

I want my children to fear the Lord, to understand there are consequences for their choices, that obedience brings blessings and disobedience, brings consequences [curses]. It is for their future welfare that I spank them when they need it. I make no apologies for that, because that is what God's Word tells me to do.

He who spares the rod hates his son. But he who loves him disciplines him diligently. [Proverb 13:22]

Dads, if we love our kids we are going to spank them. But, <u>the key to administering a spanking is to never do it in anger</u>. If you find yourself angry and spanking, *stop* until you can control that anger. If you know you are angry, just tell your children to go to their room and you will come and talk to them later [when you calm down].

In our home, we have a white paddle for spankings. When I spank, I do it once and if the rebellion has left once is enough. But there are times when I've had to administer more than one swat to see the rebellion leave. After I spank, then I hug them.

The key to discipline is attitude—ours and theirs.

Fathers, you need to be firm, fair, and loving. Not cruel, brutal and angry.

Sometimes one of my kids will try to defend his position, to basically say I'm wrong and he's right. I give him the freedom of my counting to three for him to change his attitude. I tell him "It's your choice. I need to hear a better attitude or you get another spanking." I've never had to go past three loving spankings before there was a miraculous change in attitude! My children are learning that there are consequences for behavior.

Another lesson spanking provides is to teach your child you are the parent and you are in control. They're kids, they're foolish, they're going to do things that make you angry. But you are the parent, and you need to be in control. Don't spank until you are under control.

Responsibility # 4:   Communicate love and commitment to our children.

We can communicate in three ways: verbally, by touch and by spending time [I'm going to address "time" as a separate responsibility].

Kids thrive on hearing how much we love them, how proud we are of them, how happy we are to be their father. But try to say more than, "I'm proud of you." Tell them why. They want to know. Once my daughter, Mindy, asked me, "Dad, why are you proud of me?" So I pointed out to her that I am proud of how she treats her sister, what a good friend she is, how she does her homework, on and on. That blessed her.

When you tell your children you are proud of them, give them some reasons why. Build them up. Communicate by caring and taking the time to say that you love them. When you affirm your children, they hear "Honey, I love you." If you fail to affirm them, they hear, "Dad doesn't love me anymore."

Build up your children whenever possible. Catch them doing a good job and compliment them. "I'm so proud that you finished that. I'm so proud that you didn't give up. You completed the task. That quality of finishing a job will help make you a success in your life. Good job."

Hug your kids. Hold their hands and rub their backs. Wrestle with them. Tickle them until they surrender. Put your arm around your child while you are walking. Lightly smother their faces with tiny kisses.

Responsibility # 5:   Bless your children.

Much has been written over the last decade about the importance of blessing our children, and there are many biblical examples of this.

We bless our kids by pronouncing a successful future over them.

We bless our kids by recognizing the gifts in their lives, and attaching value to them, saying things like "God is going to use that quality to bless others."

We bless our kids through our prayers with them. I literally put my hand on their heads and bless them, telling them how God is going to use them. One day my daughter said, "Dad, God has a great plan for my life. I know, I know." Obviously, Mindy has heard me tell her that fact more than once, so I replied, "That's absolutely right. God is going to use you! And I'm praying that you marry a godly man. I'm praying that you're in the ministry in some way." I just went on and on. "I don't know if you're going to marry a pastor or a carpenter, but God is going to use you and your husband some day."

I have prayed a blessing over my kids hundreds of times!

Unfortunately, God's laws are democratic, so the opposite is also true. We can curse our kids. We curse them when we say things like, "That's stupid. You're stupid. You're never going to amount to anything. You can't be a child of mine, I knew you couldn't do it," on and on.

174

Dads, we must take responsibility to bless our children, verbally pronouncing a successful [godly] future for their lives.

Responsibility # 6:   Spend time with your kids.

There is some truth to the old saying, "Spend quality time, not quantity time." Through the years, in my observations of successful families, it does appear there is some truth to spending quality time with your children. I've seen dads spend enormous amounts of time as soccer coaches, Little League coaches, etc., without building relationships.

Your goal is to build a relationship so your children will embrace your godly value system. The time with our kids is best utilized when we try to build and deepen relationship with them.

As I have observed fathers, it frequently seemed that the kids who were on fire for Jesus had dads who were extremely busy, so I knew they couldn't spend enormous amounts of time with their kids. Yet, their kids were embracing their value system. As I spoke with them, I learned that these dads took out special time out on a regular basis for each one of their children. They sometimes took them on ministry trips, or out for a one-on-one meal.

Before you know it, your kid is going to be attending 8th grade graduation, then high school and college. Before you know it you will be attending their wedding. So, make "quality time" for your kids now.

There is no greater privilege than being a father, but a father does have responsibilities. Each of us as fathers must fear God and choose to create a wealth of spiritual blessing for our children.

If we will strive to do this our children will be blessed with self-esteem, marry the right persons, know success in all areas of life, and be an example for Christ in their generation.

CHAPTER ELEVEN

Four Responsibilities of a Mother

In this chapter, I have asked four mothers I deeply respect to share on four biblical responsibilities of a mother: 1] Loving and Respecting your Husband, 2] Loving the Children, 3] Setting the Tone of the Home, and 4] Training the Children.

Loving and Respecting Your Husband

By Mary Hoffman [my wife!]

By God's grace I have come from a place of despising my husband [Dave shared this in an earlier chapter] to loving and appreciating the uniquely gifted man God has given me. My change of heart did not come by chance. It took choosing to submit to God's plan for me and our marriage.

Ephesians 5:33 commands a wife to respect her husband.

A wife must see to it that she respects her husband.

Once you marry your husband, once you make that commitment before God, you are bound by God's Word to make the best marriage possible and respect your husband.

Titus 2:5 gives us the first reason why we should respect our husbands: so the Word of God is not dishonored.

- Be subject to your own husband so that the word of God will not be dishonored.

The <u>second reason</u> for respecting your children's father is :

- Your children will learn submission to authority through your example.

If they see you love and respect their father, they will follow, and will find it easier to love and respect God.

God says He hates divorce for a good reason...it is the ultimate expression of disunity. But if a divorce must take place, the goal should be to manifest as much unity as possible with your husband for the benefit of the children. Of course, God is not saying that you must respect a wife beater or a chronic drug abuser. But, just know that your children will be harmed if you continually complain about your husband's faults in front of them. Many children internalize ungodly thoughts such as, "If my Dad is lazy and selfish, then what about me?" Even if your husband abandoned you, it is best to let the children come to their own conclusions about his ungodly behavior.

Your response is always the same: love your children enough to set the example of forgiveness and trust in the Lord. Whether married or divorced, if you have contempt for your children's father, confess that and ask the Lord to help you cultivate respect. In Psalm 50:23, God said,

Whoever offers praise glorifies me and to him who orders his conduct aright I will show the salvation of God.

And in 1 John 3:10, we learn:

In this the children of God and the children of the devil are manifested, whoever does not practice righteousness is not of God nor is he who does not love his brother.

I thank the Lord I have never experienced divorce. My parents have been married for 45 years and their example gave me the courage I needed to seek counseling rather than a lawyer when times became difficult in my own marriage. Through counseling I learned to practice the things that have greatly benefited my marriage with Dave.

I began to pray that God would help me to understand the unique personality of my husband.

For instance, Dave and I got along much better when I realized I needed to feed him consistently, and that he liked a variety of foods. Frankly, I could have lived my whole life eating nothing but breakfast cereal and chicken, but God gave me a man who likes corned beef, sauerkraut and home-made chocolate cake. Dave feels loved when I spend the day creating a great meal for him. So, I had to sacrifice my desire to never open a cookbook. After much practice I began to really enjoy cooking for my family and friends. Many times I did not want to do it for Dave, but I could always do it for the Lord.

One of the best books I have read on understanding my husband is *The Five Languages of Love*. After I read that book, I began to understand my husband better, and was more equipped to be his helpmate. Man's greatest need beside the relationship with his Heavenly Father is to have a family to care for. Being a helpmate means you make it easy for your husband to love and care for you. Tell him often you need and appreciate his help. Praise him for working hard, and for his help with the children. Encourage him through his failures.

There are many stories of God's encouragement in the Bible. My favorite is the story of Gideon in Judges, chapter 6. Imagine, Gideon was hiding from his enemies when God called him a valiant warrior!

Romans 4:17b says,

> *Our God gives life to the dead and calls things that are not as though they were.*

Then Proverb 14:1 declares,

> *The wise woman builds her house but the foolish tears it down with her own hands.*

It is easy to see your husband's faults, but it is a woman who is ruled by fear who feels compelled to always point them out. A wise woman seeks to build up her husband with prayer and encouragement.

Place your faith and trust in God to make your husband the father he needs to be for your children. A mother who respects her husband needs to practice doing what Colossians 3:8 says:

Put aside anger, wrath, jealousy, slander, and abusive speech from your mouth.

Then we are told in verse 12,

...so those who have been chosen of God, holy and beloved, put on the heart of compassion, kindness, humility, gentleness and patience; bearing with one another and forgiving each other, whoever has a complaint against anyone, just as the Lord forgave you so also should you. Beyond all these things put on love which is the perfect bond of unity.

God does not give us the luxury of complaining about our marriages. I needed to learn to identify and confess anger, bad attitudes and unrealistic expectations because I wanted to obey God's command to love and respect my husband. To help me learn those qualities, the Lord led me to a wise older woman who had a great marriage and was committed to the success of my marriage. At the beginning of our relationship I would go to her home weekly and share my anger and frustrations with her. She would always point me back to my responsibilities to minister to and love Dave, regardless of how I was feeling.

Occasionally I still get angry, but now I have learned how to obey God's command to not let the sun go down on my anger. A woman who respects and honors her husband gives her children the blessing of parents who are working together to achieve a common goal rather than competing to see who will win an argument.

Dave and I do not often agree on anything...at first. I have learned that it is far better to listen to his ideas instead of attacking them just because his ideas are different than mine. 1 John 4:8 says,

There is no fear in love but perfect love casts out fear because fear involves punishment and the one who fears is not perfected in love.

I love the song we sing in church called "Surrender." It is a great example of how to respect your children's father by giving up your rights, your dreams, and your pride so that God is free to create a miracle that is better than you had ever hoped for.

Loving the Children

By Kitty Belsey

Don't all mothers already love their children? They are so darling; you just want to kiss them.

Well, we do not always love our children. Some mothers need to be taught how to love their kids.

Titus 2:4 says,

> *Encourage the younger women to love their husbands and to love their children.*

When I first read that, I said, "Lord I receive that message. I want to learn how." Then God replied, "Kitty, you are one of the older women and you need to be teaching the younger women how to love their children. The kind of love I am asking mothers to manifest to their children is not necessarily natural."

> *Can a woman forget her nursing child? Can she feel no love for a child she has born?* [Isaiah 49:15]

In over 20 years of being a mother, I admit that there have been plenty of times when I felt a deep, abiding, joyous love for my three children. But, there have been occasional times over the past 20 years when I have felt moments of extreme frustration and anger. So, I prayed, "Lord, since I've experienced such extremes, how can I encourage women to love their children for Jesus' sake?" Through my prayer and petition, God reminded me of four practical P's a mother needs to fulfill her duty to love her children.

1)   Provide and Protect

> *If anyone does not provide for his own, especially for those of his own household, he has denied the faith and is worse than an unbeliever. [1 Timothy 5:8]*

181

One basic, obvious duty a mother has is to provide food, clothing, shelter and hygiene for their children. At a deeper level of providing and protecting them is the idea of sacrificial love [agape love] for our children. That love is not based on how we feel about our kids, or how lovable they are, but it is based on the principle that through Christ we can do all things who strengthens us. Through Christ, we can even love the sometimes unlovable child whom we are called to love sacrificially.

In 1 Kings 3:16-27 we see Solomon faced with a serious situation. Two women both claim that a particular child is theirs. Solomon listens to their dispute, then essentially says, "Bring me a sword. I will cut this child in half and give half of the child to each of you." One of the women shouts out, "No, don't do that! I give up the child. Let her raise him so he can live." Immediately Solomon knew who the real mother was: the one willing to give up her right to raise the child. The real mother gave up her desires, hopes and dreams for the sake of the child.

That woman sets an example of how we should be...mothers loving sacrificially. As we grow in our fear of the Lord, we may be called upon by God to give up something dear to us so our child will thrive and survive, for example, a hobby, recreation, social event, etc.

Sacrificial love can challenge you to a difficult, sometimes unpopular choice to remove your child from a destructive situation, be it a school your child is attending, or friendships destructive to your child. A mother who loves and fears God, and loves her child, will do the tough thing and remove that child from the destructive situation. We must make sure our kids are safe.

2)   Pray, Present and Plan

This topic is like three P's in one...sort of a trinity of P's. Hannah is a great biblical example in this area. When Samuel was born, Hannah prayed a wonderful prayer for him in Chapter one of 1 Samuel:

> *For this boy I prayed, and the Lord has given me my petition which I asked of him. So I have also dedicated him to the Lord; as long as he lives, he is dedicated to the Lord.*

182

Hannah prayed, dedicating and bringing her child to God. She submitted to God's plan for Samuel, not Hannah's plan, because she had been barren for a long time. When God finally gave her a child, I am sure the temptation was to keep him close to her, to not let him out of her sight. But Hannah knew God had a bigger plan for her son, and she submitted to that plan.

The result? At the end of Samuel's life, he addressed the leaders of Israel and declared:

Since my childhood on I have served God and I haven't defrauded any one of you. [1 Samuel. 12:3]

In essence, Samuel was saying, "I never felt the need to experiment with sin." He had a great testimony! Isn't that what you want for your children? I want my kids to be able to say, "From my childhood I have loved God and had a mother who prayed for me."

Luke 18 tells us about moms who brought their children to Jesus. Crowds were all around Him, and many put demands on Him, but these moms pushed through the crowds because they were determined: nothing was going to stop them.

Every time we bring a child to church, or pray with a child, we are bringing Christ to the child or the child to Christ. That is our solemn duty.

In Luke 1, we read about Mary, the mother of Jesus. Chapters one and two provide an example of a woman who receives a Word from God that she is going to have a child. She received a definite plan for this child's life. She pondered the message in her heart, then replied,

Behold the bond slave of the Lord. Be it done to me according to your will. [Luke 1:38]

She didn't say, "Hey, wait a second, you mean to tell me I am going to have a child? Well, if that's the case, there are things I want this child to accomplish."

Instead, Mary submitted her will for this child's life to God's will, committing her whole life to God's plan. In Chapter two Mary brings Jesus to the temple to present Him to the Lord. Jesus was schooled in scripture, and at age twelve He was able to converse with great wisdom with the elders on scripture.

The child continued to grow and become strong. He increased in wisdom and the grace of God was upon him.

Jesus was a well-adjusted individual who showed balanced growth in the four major stages of development that every child needs to go through: physical [He grew in stature], mental [He grew in wisdom and knowledge], social [He grew in favor with man], and spiritual [He grew in favor with God].

That is our desire for our children...to live balanced, healthy lives.

3)   Pay attention

Your children need you to pay attention. I asked my children, "What is the main responsibility I have to you?" They told me, "You need to listen to us!" That answer surprised me. Sometimes I do not always understand what they are saying because I am so busy. But not listening? One of my children told me, "Mom you never listen to me."

Granted, I do not always hear exactly the words my children say to me, but I was surprised they all agreed I needed to be a better listener. So, I asked the Holy Spirit to be my hearing aid, helping me hear what the child is really saying and needing. Each day I pray, "Lord please interpret for me what my child is saying and what he needs for me to hear."

And the Holy Spirit is faithful.

Deborah was a wise counselor and listener. In Chapter 4 of Judges, we see the sons of Israel come to Deborah, who was a judge and a mother to all of Israel. They would come to her with their problems. She would listen to what they said, take her time reaching a decision, then give wise counsel and direction. We need to be that kind of loving mother and judge for our children.

4)   Be a "pillow"

Be as soft and comforting as the pillow your child sleeps on. Your child needs your unwavering tenderness and affection. Titus challenges us to be a child-lover, tender and affectionate and constant [not hot and cold]. Your child needs to know you are consistent and genuine. Psalm 131:2 and Isaiah 66:12-13 describe how a mother's touch composes and quiets a child.

One of *The Five Languages of Love* is touch. Ever since my children were little, I have made a point of touching and scratching their backs, playing with their hair, hugging them daily.

One of my children is at an age where a physical touch is "like un-cool." I need to respect that, but the Holy Spirit has told me that this child still needs contact with his Mom. Recently I noticed this child bouncing a basketball listlessly, waiting for Dad to come home so they could shoot some hoops. Because I knew he could use some attention, I said, "Would you like me to shoot some hoops with you?" to which he lovingly replied, "You?"

He stared at my skinny little arms, and he knows that I am pretty uncoordinated. "Sure! I'll shoot some hoops with you," he replied. When I gave him my best moves, and started making some baskets, he said, "Hey, you can actually get it in the hoop!" We kind of looked at each other and smiled, then played for about 45 minutes. He didn't know it at the time, but I was hugging him through shooting hoops. God gave me a way to still have contact with him.

Ezekiel 16.44-45 gives an example of when a mother loathes her children.

> *Behold, everyone who quotes proverbs will quote this proverb concerning you, saying, 'Like mother, like daughter. You are the daughter of your mother, who loathed her husband and children. You are also the sister of your sisters, who loathed their husbands and children. Your mother was a Hittite and your father an Amorite.*

Mothers, never communicate loathing, despising, contempt. Your children take it in and "like mother, like daughter" you will teach it to your children who will pass it on to their children as a major generational curse.

When you feel, "I can't love this kid!" remember that you can through Christ who strengthens you. You can love the unlovable. Your children must have a deep heart knowledge, a genuine, unshakable love in you.

1 Corinthians 13:1-3 gives us a real practical way of loving. As you read it, ask the Lord, "Show me how to love this child. Help me to not treat my child in a way that destroys him or tears him down. Help me not to be rude or harsh with my child."

If I speak with the tongues of men and of angels, but do not have love, I have become a noisy gong or a clanging cymbal.

If I have the gift of prophecy, and know all mysteries and all knowledge; and if I have all faith, so as to remove mountains, but do not have love, I am nothing.

And if I give all my possessions to feed the poor, and if I surrender my body to be burned, but do not have love, it profits me nothing. [1 Corinthians 13:1-3]

Setting the Tone of the Home
By Nancy Matthews

A woman who fears the Lord shall be praised and respected. [Proverbs 31:30b]

I love praise, a pat on the back, someone who says, "Good job." I want to be a woman who fears the Lord in such a way that I do an excellent job as a mom.

Our children follow by example. John 13:15 says,

I have set you an example that you should do as I have done for you.

I want my children to follow the example of Christ. In my section, I am going to list a few of the examples I want my children to follow.

Contentment

A mom can set the tone of the household, manifesting contentment no matter what the current circumstances are. Moms help set the overall satisfaction level of our home by teaching contentment.

We are not born content. If you think that's not true, you've never heard a screaming baby. Paul says in Philippians 4:11-13,

> *Not that I speak in respect of want: for I have learned, in whatsoever state I am, therewith to be content. I know both how to be abased, and I know how to abound: every where and in all things I am instructed both to be full and to be hungry, both to abound and to suffer need. I can do all things through Christ which strengtheneth me.*

As wives and mothers, we need to be satisfied in all things, including the income level our husbands provide; we need to learn to live within those means and adapt to our circumstances. Sometimes money is tight, and our children need to hear, "No, we cannot afford to go to the movies this weekend. We need to stick to a budget." If Mom is content with what she has, and does not complain, her children will follow her example.

We made a choice to send our children to Christian schools. So, I drive an old car from my husband's grandmother because I want to show the kids that life is about choices. Moses chose to suffer affliction rather than give in to earthly pleasures.

> *Choosing rather to suffer affliction with the people of God, than to enjoy the pleasures of sin for a season;*
> *[Hebrews 11:25]*

Budget

Live within your means. Try hard to stay out of debt.

187

I want my household to rest in contentment, to love life, and be debt free. I also want my children to understand that sometimes troubles will come their way, but that God will always give us the strength to see us through those troubles.

Household Basics

Clean House, Good Dinner, Great Conversations, Stewardship, Self-Discipline and Organizational Skills.

If you look at the Proverbs 31 woman, most of us would say "There is no way I could be like that super woman!" Well, the first step is to strive for basics—a clean house and a good dinner on the table. When you provide a sit-down dinner for your family, giving them a nutritious meal that has taken time to prepare, the atmosphere stirs good conversations [sometimes even heated discussions] which help bind a family together. I learned from my parents' example. We had dinner together as a family at least five nights a week, and we always celebrated holidays around the dinner table.

A clean house shows your children stewardship, self-discipline and organizational skills [and they will follow by your example]. My motto has always been, "Stay organized so you can have fun later in the day." When my children were young, my sisters and I used to live by this code: "Get up, get the house cleaned, start your dinner preparations by 10 a.m., then let the kids play with each other while we [the sisters] changed the world with our conversations."

As my children grew, and I had more time available, I was able to work outside of my home. This again required me to demonstrate to my children how to organize time.

Hospitality

Well reported of for good works; if she have brought up children, if she have lodged strangers, if she have washed the saints' feet, if she have relieved the afflicted, if she have diligently followed every good work.

[1 Timothy 5:10]

This wife was well known for her good deeds such as bringing up her children, showing hospitality, washing the feet of the saints, helping those in trouble, and devoting herself to good deeds.

Many women fear hospitality, and that limits their willingness to open up their homes to others. Hospitality is simply the gathering together of friends and family in an atmosphere of love. It has nothing to do with settings of silver or fancy dinners, but is rather an invisible "welcome" sign that radiates from your heart attitude. My home is known as "the revolving door." It seems someone is always living with us or visiting. We love to help people by providing a place to stay. My parents did the same. There were seven kids in our family, yet my parents would always open our home to friends and family who needed a place. My mom would say, "What's one more?" Over my lifetime my grandma, my great grandma, my aunts and my cousins all lived with us at one time or another.

Mom and Dad gave me the heritage of the gift of hospitality. Because of their example, I have opened my home to friends and family. Pastor John Hoffman says his mom was known as "the Kool Aid and cookie Mom." What an excellent opportunity to speak into your children's friends lives.

We need to be cheerleaders for our kids and for their friends.

Training Your Children
By Linda Hoffman

Train up a child in the way he should go and even when he is old he will not depart from it. [Proverb 22:6]

Some will ask, "How do you train your children in all the ways they should go?" Others will say, "I trained up my child and they departed." My question to you would be, "Are you *telling* them or *training* them?"

To *tell* is to explain in words, to inform, to give an account. Do you read your child a Bible study at bedtime, pat them on the head, kiss them good night and leave the room?

To *train* is to direct the growth, to form it by instruction and drill, to teach by being qualified and proficient in that area, and to be prepared for a test of its skill.

We are required to train, not tell.

If my son was going into the Army and was going to war, I would expect the Army to train him, not tell him, what he is going to encounter. If they just tell my son, he will be unprepared to go to battle, and we would need to prepare for his death. I want my son trained! I want my son to receive direction and teaching that will prepare him for a test of his skill.

There are two very necessary skills in training up a child for the battle of life:

> Skill One: Form in them an appetite for the things of God.
>
> Skill Two: Train them in self-control.

If you can teach your child these two things, they will have success in life.

An appetite for God means that they are trained to love that which is true, good, right, just, excellent and of good report [see Philippians 4:8]. They must like the places where God is, where His Word is taught; they must develop an appetite to like His people. It is my responsibility to make sure our children are in the place where they will feel His nearness, love and guidance.

The things of God are not just told, they are formed, taught and directed.

Our church has cultivated a youth culture where it is cool to love God. We have camps and retreats to divert the attention of our youth from the things of the world and back to the things of God. The kids have learned how to worship, to repent, and to experience reform in their hearts in the presence of their King. At a recent Future Quest youth outreach, I witnessed hundreds of youth with their hands raised up and not one of them was embarrassed in front of their friends. Another time I saw a young grandmother with her two-year-old grandchild with her hands lifted up in the air, modeling what was naturally happening to everyone around her.

We need to cultivate an appetite for God! Do you restrict your child from the things of God when they get into trouble? Restrict them from soccer, restrict them from their friends, restrict them from the telephone, but not from youth camp [even if it is fun]. These camps are purposely made to be fun so your child will come and experience God.

Next, train them up in self-control.

You can train them in two very different ways: 1] you can nag them, or 2] teach them to control themselves.

Most would agree that it is better to opt for teaching children to control themselves, but how do you do that? Well, to answer that, I need to have you answer four questions:

1] What do you do when you see a character fault in your child?
2] What character do you want to see?
3] How do you discourage what you do not want to see?
4] How do you encourage what you want to see?

One day my kids were playing with some neighbors, and one of their friends kept using antagonistic words likely to start a fight.

1] I saw and heard these unkind words.
2] What did I want to see? Kind words.
3] How do I discourage the unkind?
4] How could I encourage the kind?

As I was in the kitchen asking myself these questions, I heard this child in the other room calling his fellow cherubs "liars." When I called this to his attention, he said he did not even know he was doing it. So I encouraged him to "Stop saying that." A few minutes later I again said, "Stop saying that." Then, a few minutes later I thought, "This isn't working. Unless he wants to stop this, it is an exercise in futility."

My next brainstorm was to "time him." In the next 90 seconds he said "liar" 21 times. I then walked into the living room, armed with what I was sure was relevant information, and asked him, "Do you know how many times you've said liar?" "No." "You said it 21 times in 90 seconds!" "Li- -," he started to say, stopping himself. "I mean, I did not."

That was the start of some self-control. Then I thought I would make it worth his while to catch himself, since it was not working for me to catch him. I thought, "What do kids want?" Candy! "Listen, I'll make a deal with you. I will buy a big bag of candy and put your name on it. Nobody can touch it but you. Every day that you do not say liar, not even once, I am going to let you come to my house, put your hand in that bag and pull out as much candy as you can get."

His sister immediately piped up, "I have bad habits too, you know."

The very next moment this boy turned to his friend as they continued the game called one a "Li—," stopping without completing the "ar." The others yelled, "He said it. He said it!" I replied, "No he didn't. He stopped himself, so that one doesn't count."

Well, the boy didn't get a handful of candy that day, but within two weeks he had completely stopped saying "Liar," and to my knowledge, does not say it anymore. He learned self-control, which is much better than me nagging him.

If I love and fear God, His Word must be written on the heart of my kids. They must be trained in self-control, a different task for each of the four basic stages of growth. Let me share in a bit of detail how each stage requires a different approach.

Stage One: Zero Through Four Years

The first stage of growth is zero to four years when they are just learning to bond. In this stage, they need stability and regularity in their lives. They need to be hugged and loved by the same people on a regular basis. The best stability grows when they know who is going to watch over them, day in and day out. They need to know who is going to put the Band-Aid on, who will hold them when they have a fever, who will applaud them when they take their first steps. They need to know that you were chosen by God to baby-sit for them.

As a first priority, give them stability and regularity. After you are steadily doing that, only then do you begin to fill up your life with all those other things the world says you have to have. If you are a single mom, someone will need to take care of your child while you work to provide a living for him. Even in this situation, always strive to give the child as much stability as possible. Studies prove that a home atmosphere where one adult is caring for a small group of children produces the strongest children.

This is also the stage where little Johnny or Debra begins to learn self-control, which, at this stage, I define as obedience without understanding. Whether they understand or not, they cannot touch the stove! Whether they understand it or not, they cannot go out into the street, hit their mom, or talk back. I'll always explain the good reasons why I make the demands I do, but my children must obey even if they do not understand or agree with my explanations. If you are lenient and permissive here, then their will is only going to grow stronger, and self-control will be harder and more costly in the next stage.

Stage Two: Five to Eleven

At this age children need to belong in the family, receive parental approval, master the basic skills of life, and learn to function with others. I want them to be loved and welcomed in their friends' homes, and I want them to be likeable to others. So, I am going to train them to say "please," "thank you," and "forgive me." I am going to teach them to share their toys [which they never want to do], and teach them to give their front seat to a brother or a friend [this is their first taste of unselfish love]. Scripture tell us, "If a man wants friends, he must show himself friendly." So, I am going to teach and train them to be friendly, to have manners, politeness, and cleanliness.

I must teach them that the Word of God is true, so turning the other cheek is not a weakness but gives them the greatest power of all. They can turn their enemy into a friend. Anyone can aggravate and antagonize their enemy, but I teach them how to have the power to turn an enemy into a friend. I also teach them that God in heaven is for justice, so when an injustice is perpetrated against them, they will be taught not to respond in fury and hostility because they know that their God is the avenger of the oppressed.

If I train them in His Word, when unfairness befalls them they may become angry but they will not resort to violence. They will get sad but it will not grow into depression. They will be hurt but it will not breed hostility and vengeance because they have been taught that goodness triumphs over evil. They will start to become the sons of their Father who is in heaven. I must train them to discern what is good and evil, what is genuine and counterfeit, and then to prefer the good to the evil.

Children are trained first by watching you. They will not rise much above what you do and believe. We must plug the leaks in the home by monitoring what they watch on TV, monitoring what game they are playing on Nintendo, monitoring what videos and movies they can watch. They will dream about what they see and hear the most. When my son was on the couch the other day I asked, "What are you thinking?" He was thinking about the last movie he watched. Wherever the leaks are, that is what keeps the desire for immoral things alive in the hearts of our kids, and the things of God grow strangely dim. You cannot love what is good if evil is always before you.

Proverbs 22:15 declares that...

Foolishness is bound in the heart of a child; but the rod of correction shall drive it far from him.

Yes, our children are supposed to be little fools, but the rod of discipline will eventually remove the foolishness from them.

While you are administering discipline, do not lose heart for in due time you will reap if you do not faint.

Stage Three: Twelve to Fourteen

These are the years of alignment, when a child forms and accepts a philosophy and starts aligning himself with a particular group. They start to realize what they are good at, and say things such as "I am a basketball player," or "I am a scholar," or "I am a Christian." I want my kids to say, "I am a Christian, and by the way, I play basketball." I want them to say, "I am a Christian, and by the way I'm in a band that's going on tour."

The power of a parent is the ability to choose who will influence our children.

What school are you sending them to? Do you know who their teachers are, and what they are saying to your child? What about their activities outside the home?

When I was about fifteen, I wanted to go to a concert with some questionable friends who were not overflowing with moral excellence. As I tried to explain to my mother the benefits of my going, she said, "I do not think so, honey." She was chopping lettuce in the kitchen as I began to expound on why she wasn't seeing things correctly. Again, she said "No, honey." She kept chopping lettuce and I kept on arguing. "No, honey," again was her reply. Finally I threw up my hands, stomped out of the room and said, "Why do I even ask?" And very quietly in the background I heard her say, "*That* is a good question."

Teach your kids how to choose their friends based upon whether they are good for them or not. If you become careless or thoughtless in this task, it will cost you greatly. Do not assume everything is fine with your child just because they are doing well in school. Curfews are a good discipline. Chores are a good discipline. Mandatory youth group attendance is a good discipline. Proverbs 19:18 says,

Discipline your son while there is hope and do not desire his death.

195

Another version says:

Discipline your son while there is hope and do not set your heart on their destruction.

But my favorite version is the King James:

Discipline your son while there is hope and do not refrain from discipline because of his loud crying.

Stage Four: Fifteen through Eighteen

These are the years of identification. They are already aligned now, and they begin to identify and own the things of the group that they have aligned with. This is where you reap what you sow. You cannot reap what you have not sown. If you have only *told* them the truth they might not buy into it. But, if you have *trained* them, they will struggle through their sin and eventually come out on the right side of the battle.

At this point they will have made a decision to identify with a group. "The athletes wanted and accepted me so that is what I am." "The stoners wanted and accepted me so I chose their way of life." "The evolutionists had a better argument for life than my parents, so I chose to pattern my life after their philosophy and thinking."

But, if you have trained them, they will struggle through their sin and eventually come out on the right side of the battle. That's the fruit of the training: love, joy, peace, patience, kindness, goodness, and self-control. They will be well-liked, welcomed into their friends' homes, confident [because they know they can control the worries and fears coming at them]. They will believe that God is for them, and they will walk in confidence that He directs their path. Train them in the way that they should go and when they are old they will not depart from Him.

As a mother who has learned to fear the Lord, I can say "He promised it and I believe it."

CHAPTER TWELVE

Fearing God by Loving Others

A new commandment I give to you that you love one another. Even as I have loved you that you also love one another. By this all men will know that you are my disciples if you have love for one another. [John 13:34-35]

Obeying Jesus' command to *"love one another"* is a central issue when you choose to fear the Lord. It is especially important to love those in the Body of Christ...the brethren. God's plan for His people certainly includes loving neighbors [Mark 12:31] and enemies [Luke 6:27] but loving other Christians is the priority. I believe the reason for this is when you learn to love the brethren it becomes easier to love your neighbors and enemies.

The instruction to love one another occurs fifty-five times in the New Testament. Love among believers is so important that Jesus made this a special issue:

A new commandment I give to you that you love one another. Even as I have loved you that you also love one another. By this all men will know that you are my disciples if you have love for one another. [John 13:34-35]

According to Jesus you are testifying to others that you belong to Him when you love the brethren.

A Desire Rooted in God

Love among believers is supposed to attract the world's attention primarily because God is living in the hearts of all who receive Him. It is simply not church buildings, programs, and preaching that draw the world to Jesus. Those things are good...even important...but the supernatural love displayed between brothers and sisters in Christ is what woos people of the world! It is one of the key differences between Christianity and other religions and philosophies.

Beloved, let us love one another, for love is from God; and everyone who loves is born of God and knows God. The one who does not love does not know God, for God is love. Beloved, if God so loved us, we also ought to love one another. No one has seen God at any time; if we love one another, God abides in us, and His love is perfected in us. By this we know that we abide in Him and He in us, because He has given us His Spirit. [1 John 4:7-8,11-13]

Please do not miss the immensity of what John says in this scripture. If you have even a minute desire to love the brethren that is proof that God's Spirit is living in you! God is love. A desire to love other believers is an undeniable testimony that you know God and are born again.

And this commandment we have from Him, that the one who loves God should love his brother also. Whoever believes that Jesus is Christ is born of God, and whoever loves the Father loves the child born of Him.

[1 John 4:21-5:1]

When you give your life to Jesus Christ the Spirit of the Lord takes up residency inside you and you become a child of God. Those who love God will also love His children, so you can expect to love others who have the same Spirit of the Lord residing in them. Quite literally, God's Spirit in you loves God's Spirit in them!

An Impossible Dream...*Without Jesus!*

...everyone who loves is born of God and knows God.
[1 John 4:7b]

A person who is *not* born again and does *not* have God's Spirit residing within is *not* capable of biblical supernatural love! Love is not possible for them because God...*Who is love*...Who is the source of all love...is not present in them. Yet they were created with the desire to love and be loved and that is why love among the brethren is so attractive to them. It is what they desperately need and do not have. The supernatural love among believers is a divine invitation to a loveless world.

I was part of the generation during the late 1960's and early 1970's that thought we could bring a revolution of love and peace to the world. We believed a new reality in the world was on the horizon...the oneness of *mankind*. We were not citizens of the United States but citizens of the world. Borders were meaningless. People everywhere were members of one family...humanity...and the only way to survive and thrive was to embrace each other in love! Our music and literature affirmed these ideas. Yet within a relatively short time this movement died. Why? I believe it was because as we grew up a bit and experienced life we discovered that we were not capable of loving others! We were a generation completely surrendered to selfishness. One reason we rejected the values and morals of our parents is because we wanted to have our own way and abandon ourselves to our desires and whims. When the philosophy of love and peace was introduced it seemed to accommodate those selfish pursuits so we embraced it. Yet not everyone we encountered was lovable. Many were not even likable. To love them would have required self-sacrifice...the antithesis of a self-centered, self-indulging generation. We only wanted to love people if it was easy. It was not!

Friend, the only way a human can consistently love others is to allow Christ to love through them. Regardless of culture, environment or ethnicity we are all selfish. We need something larger...a power greater than ourselves...to overcome selfishness.

A Mark Upon the Heart

Fearing God means obeying Him. It is clear in His Word that loving one another in the church is not an option...it is a command to be obeyed.

> *If someone says, 'I love God,' and hates his brother, he's a liar; for the one who does not love his brother whom he has seen, cannot love God whom he has not seen.*
>
> *[1 John 4:20]*

199

You cannot love God and despise His people. I understand some people are difficult to love. Yet the most disagreeable believer is precious to God because His Spirit dwells within!

Christian means *little Christ*. Every believer is a little Christ! (I do not mean that believers are God, but that God dwells in each believer making that person the representation of Christ to others.) A person cannot love Christ without also loving His people because it is really Christ in them you are loving.

The one who joins himself to the Lord is one spirit with Him. [1 Corinthians 6:17]

Let's consider what the Apostle Paul wrote about this in Galatians:

For in Christ Jesus neither circumcision nor uncircumcision means anything, but faith working through love. [Galatians 5:6]

The only thing that matters in Christian life is love. When Paul wrote this a great controversy had broken out in the church regarding whether or not new believers were to be circumcised. Circumcision was required for Jews under the old law of the covenant. Some insisted that to belong to God's family new believers must become circumcised. Essentially Paul is saying, "When the love of Jesus is in the heart, what is done to the flesh is not important! If you want the mark of circumcision for yourself— fine! But do not force your preference on others."

When Jesus fully obeyed God's law and offered Himself as an atonement for all mankind, God's people were released from the requirement of circumcision. A child of God was no longer marked by circumcision but by the presence of God's Holy Spirit in them. Paul's message to the Galatians and to us is this: "Loving your community...being a light to people in darkness...loving each other in a way that wins non-believers to Christ...is the evidence of your faith and it is through faith that you are a member of God's family, not circumcision!"

Let's consider some modern controversies. There are various beliefs that can bring division in the Body of Christ. For example, should we baptize infants or practice believers' baptism, the issue of tongues, baptism of the Holy Spirit, the seeker sensitive issue, end times theology, and the list goes on. I believe Paul's response to these issues would be the same: "These issues are not the core of our faith." What is important is what you do for Jesus in love. When the trumpet sounds I don't believe anyone of us will care about many of the issues that we now feel are so important. What will matter is what you did while you were able to impact the world for Jesus. Did you express your faith by loving people?

The Power of Love and Unity

We are blessed in the United States to have religious freedom. We have Bible bookstores, wonderful church buildings, printing presses, radio and television programs and open worship services. Imagine for a moment that this freedom was gone. Besides God, what would we have? Each other! That is a reality for many Christians around the world. Some do not have so much as a complete copy of the Bible! Yet God moves powerfully in their midst.

My brother, Mark, and I have made it a priority to know the other pastors in San Diego's East County because we understand the importance of loving others in the Body of Christ. When we come to know them, what needs they have, then...we are able to support them in love. For years we have made it a practice to pray for other churches during our weekend services. Foothills has a rich history of giving financial support to other churches.

When you find remarkable growth in the Church of Jesus Christ anywhere in the world you will also find Christians committed to loving one another. I have had the privilege of ministering in other countries and have experienced God moving powerfully. I believe the contemporary American church generally has not experienced this kind of revival because we are not known for our love of one another as commanded in scripture. When we love one another we expose our spiritual self...our light shines and people are attracted to it.

Jesus said, *"When I am lifted up I will draw all men to myself."* *[John 12:32]* Certainly He was talking about the salvation of the cross, but I believe when Christians love in the Name of Jesus, His Name is lifted up and people are drawn to Him. The biggest evangelistic tool in the church is Christians loving each other and the world around them.

Many people who have become members of Foothills did so as the result of seeing the love poured out on a friend or relative who is part of our church family. Recently an entire family was saved one Easter Sunday and the only reason they were in church was because they had seen how their neighbor...a member of Foothills...had been loved by people in our church.

The people of Foothills also showered one woman with love and support when her husband died. As a result, the woman's family now attends church. That would not have happened if the people in the church had not obeyed Christ's command to *"love one another."*

It is natural to stand with a relative who is in trouble, suffering or struggling. Yet that is not usually extended to people outside one's biological family. People are simply too selfish. Christians are able to do it because there is something inside them that *desires* to help and to love...God's Spirit.

A Costly Commandment

This is My commandment, that you love one another, just as I loved you. Greater love has no one than this, that one lay down his life for his friends. [John 15:12-13]

Loving others will most likely cost you something. It often involves a caring act or helpful provision that is to some degree inconvenient. You cannot usually plan the act of loving others:

"Okay, Sister Mary is going to have some problems next Wednesday and will need my help. I'll just schedule that right here in my day planner."

Instead, loving others will probably wreak havoc on your schedule.

This happens to me regularly. I begin my day with a list of things I want to accomplish at the office then someone calls or comes in to talk:

Pastor, can I see you? It will only take a few minutes.

My human reaction is, "You are messing with my day! And I know you will take much more than a few minutes...it will be at least an hour!" Thankfully, I have learned *not* to react from my emotion, but to respond out of the love of God's Spirit dwelling in me. I set aside my list and minister to the person in need. Remarkably, God always multiplies my time. Some of the best messages I have preached are those I did not have time to prepare because I was ministering to someone in crisis. God simply put the message together for me.

Jesus said:

If anyone wishes to come after Me, he must deny himself.
[Matthew 16:24]

Loving others requires you to deny yourself. If you have children you understand the depth of this truth.

Marriage forced me to make *some* changes in my life but the arrival of my first child forced a major shift. The second child came and messed with my life even more. By the time our third child arrived I had no life! [I'm joking here to make a point.] Few things will require you to deny yourself the way parenting does...and I can think of nothing that results in a greater blessing! When you lay down your life for your children...really put your heart and soul into them you will be blessed beyond what you can imagine!

That is also true when we love others. You may be forced to choose between helping someone or having a day to yourself for fishing, golfing or shopping.

A complaint pastors often hear is:

"I became involved in a ministry at my last church and I was burned out by it. The people there took advantage of me and I'm tired of it."

Besides having a sinful attitude, these people are completely missing the point! When you love the brethren your focus is never to be what you can gain...it is what you can do for Jesus.

Do people abuse those in ministry and church leadership? Absolutely! Some people in the church have terrible problems and are difficult to love. Often their immaturity is the reason they are having problems. They are bound to do things that offend. Loving them will help them grow and they will come to realize that they must change. Some are stubborn and refuse to grow but do not get angry at them. Simply accept that you have done what you were supposed to do and let their issue lie with them and God.

The focus must always be on Jesus when you choose to love others. Look for the Jesus in them and minister to Him! You will be blessed regardless of their response. Do not allow the enemy to cheat you out of a blessing by responding to their actions.

After winning a nuisance lawsuit, a wealthy industrialist named Charles Schwab asked the judge if he could address the people in the courtroom. He said,

"I'd like to say here in a court of law, speaking as an old man [he was seventy years old] that ninety percent of my troubles are traceable to my being kind to other people. Look young people, if you want to steer away from trouble...be hard-nosed! Be quick to say, "No!" If you follow this rule you will seldom be bothered in this life...except you'll have no friends, you'll be lonely and you won't have any fun."

I do not know if this man was a Christian but he certainly learned an important truth: the price you pay for loving others outweighs the price you pay when you do not! I've been a Christian for 27 years and a pastor for more than 20 and can testify to the fact that the Christians with the most friends...the ones who are deeply loved by others...those with the most stories to tell about God working miraculously...are those who are committed to loving the brethren.

Divine Dividends

For a wonderful example of the value that comes from investing in people's lives I need only to look to my brother, Mark. He has a greater love for young people...especially teenagers...than anyone I have ever known. Long after I would have given up on a youngster he continues to love them. At times Mark has been very discouraged...he's poured countless hours into loving and discipling a younger man only to see him stray from God and leave the church. Yet so many times, after years of being away from the Lord, these people come back. Some are in ministry. There are scores of adults who are 25...30...35 years old who say they owe their life to Mark. He poured so much of Jesus into them that they had to come back.

When finally I committed my life to Jesus Christ at age 22 I was genuinely surprised at how much of the Bible I knew. One day I was sitting in an adult Sunday school class and realized I knew more about the Bible than the teacher. My parents had used scripture to train me throughout my childhood and I attended a Christian school where we had a Bible lesson every day and I was required to memorize a Bible verse every day. I also had to memorize all of Luther's Small Catechism.

I was filled with biblical truth but also worldly values because of the previous ten years...and that resulted in serious tension in my life! The Lord brought people to minister to me who were not pastors or theologians...they were simply people who loved God, knew His Word and made themselves available to me. One of them was a woman with a son my age with whom I grew up. He had not rejected Christ, but married and moved away. She had two other children still living with her but she opened her home and her heart to me. She said I was welcome in her home any time and I took her up on it. I would drop by just to say, "Hello" and she would sit me down at the kitchen table, feed me, and talk to me for hours.

I did not realize the sacrifice that lovely woman made for me until I was older. I am certain she had a list of things to do. Sometimes as we talked she would fold baskets full of laundry.

She had a husband and the two children still living at home. I know many times that dear brother must have come home from work and dinner was not on the table because I had been there for hours. She was discipling me...loving me...the way Jesus instructs His followers to love others! She possessed a genuine love for the brethren.

Discipling is a real need in the church. Seasoned Christians give—and receive—so much when they spend time walking beside someone who is new in the Lord or experiencing difficulties. You do not have to be a theologian to disciple others...just one who attends church regularly for a couple of years and reads God's Word. You do not have to know the answers to all the questions that will come up, but you will know some answers. And when you do not know an answer you and your disciple can learn the answer together from someone who does, such as a pastor. I published this book in hopes that some of you will take this book and disciple others.

Love Is...

The Bible defines genuine love for others in 1 Corinthians 13. This passage is usually read during marriage ceremonies but it applies to loving the brethren:

> *Love is patient, love is kind and is not jealous; love does not brag and is not arrogant, does not act unbecomingly: it does not seek its own, is not provoked, does not take into account a wrong suffered, does not rejoice in unright-eousness, but rejoices with the truth; bears all things, believes all things, hopes all things, endures all things. Love never fails. [1 Corinthians 13:4-8]*

Loving a Christian brother or sister means choosing to believe that they will do the right thing...eventually. You pray and keep praying...love and keep loving. Sooner or later the person will come around. Jesus promised never to leave or forsake that person and He promised to complete the good work He began in them.

As Christians we cannot fail one another. More than anything else our unwavering support and love will demonstrate to that person...and the world...that we are the disciples of Jesus Christ. Certainly we are not perfect, but if you take one situation at a time...one person at a time...and choose to see that person as someone God wants you to love, you will be surprised how close you come to living the definition of love you just read. If you fail...*and you will*...simply ask the Lord to forgive you and try again.

One of the things I love best about being a Christian is that if I failed yesterday...it is not what matters! God cares only about today! If I failed a brother or sister certainly I need to go to them and apologize. Yet I have learned an amazing truth about these failures...when they are handled righteously they often result in a closer relationship between the people involved!

How to Love the Brethren

I am a person who prefers easy definitions and practical applications, so I have distilled the vast topic of how to love the brethren down to two basic categories:

1. Fulfilling needs.
2. Speaking the truth in love.

First, you love the brethren when you help fulfill needs. This can be done through the church by participating in ministry, assisting the staff and helping with special projects...or by helping another believer directly.

The Day of Pentecost is when believers, filled with the Holy Spirit, preached about the Lord Jesus Christ and three thousand men were saved...that is probably about ten thousand people including women and children. The book of Acts records what happened soon after:

All those who had believed were together and had all things in common; and they began selling their property and possessions and were sharing them with all, as anyone might have need. [Acts 2:44-45]

This passage makes many Christians nervous. They think it means that they must sell off all personal possessions, keep only what can be used in community, and live with other believers in a commune or cheap apartment. Not true! Serious problems can arise when one scripture is used as a basis for anything! You must look at the whole Word of God to understand the heart of any issue in scripture.

> *And the congregation of those who believed were of one heart and one soul; and not one of them claimed that anything belonging to him was his own, but all things were common property to them. [Acts 4:32]*

One of the ministries I helped start at Foothills is Crown Financial Ministries...a 10-week course teaching biblical principles for handling finances. In the first few weeks there is great emphasis placed on the fact that God owns everything. When someone becomes a Christian they surrender their life—and everything they have—to Christ. Everything belongs to God and the believer is simply to act as manager or steward. Christians should regularly ask the Lord to help them be good and wise stewards of all He has given them.

God's will is for every believer to increase what He has entrusted to them! The Bible says God expects His people to prosper. Proverbs says a wise man leaves an inheritance for his children and his children's children. The parable Jesus told of the talents in Matthew 25 specifically addresses God's expectation that believers invest and increase. Why does God want believers to increase what He has given? I believe it is so there will be an abundance to give away. Read the parable of the talents in Matthew 25:14-30 and it is obvious that God is not pleased with the one who buried his possessions in the ground. He is quite pleased with the two who invested and earned an increase.

I believe Christians hold *"all things in common"* by recognizing that everything really belongs to God and they are simply the managers. God pours out provisions through individuals in the community. When He illuminates a need in the Body the individual believer's responsibility is to use the provisions under their care to supply the needs of others in church. The faithful steward can be certain that God will supply any need they may experience as a result of their obedience to give. No doubt you have heard it said time and time again: you cannot out–give God!

It is important to prayerfully seek God's direction when you have the means to alleviate the suffering or hardship of someone in the church. God does not desire His people to fill every need that emerges as a rote response. Only He knows what is really at work in the situation and it is only through prayerfully seeking His direction that you will know how to respond. Sometimes God will want you to fill the need you see, but other times He will want you to be only part of His provision or simply commit to intercession on their behalf.

Perhaps the need is monetary and in order to obey God in your finances you have only a small amount to share. You should share what you have and ask the Lord to provide the rest through others or ask Him to give you other ideas for helping. Only God will know the best way to utilize the provision He has made through you, but if you see a need in the church...fill it!

> *But whoever has the world's goods, and sees his brother in need and closes his heart against him, how does the love of God abide in him? Little children, let us not love with word or tongue, but in deed and truth.*
> *[1 John 3:17-18]*

Love is an action. It involves giving and doing. If you honestly are not able to fill a need, get on your knees and ask God to provide laborers for the work. Perhaps you can give your time. Simply listening and being a friend like the woman who loved me as a new Christian, or offering to watch someone's children are other ways of helping with needs.

Perhaps you have only $35.00 to share and you know of a family with great need. You can buy $35.00 worth of groceries, sneak up to their house, place the groceries in front of the door, ring the bell and *run*. I have done that and it is fun! When they see groceries and no one is around, guess who receives credit for leaving the groceries? God!

The second way to love the brethren is by speaking the truth in love. Jesus launched His ministry by announcing that His goal was to set captives free. Soon after, He explained that *truth* frees captives...and He is Truth! What could be more loving than helping someone find freedom through biblical truth!

Loving people in the church means you must be willing to speak the truth to them regardless of how they may receive it. Sometimes people do not want to hear truth. Often biblical truth is contrary to what is popular and acceptable in the world.

People do not always respond well to biblical truth. Many times I am prompted by the Lord to speak truths to people who do not want to hear it. I am certain some think, "Who does he think he is...telling me this?" Speaking the truth is confrontational!

Brethren, even if anyone is caught in any trespass, you who are spiritual, restore such a one in a spirit of gentleness; each one looking to yourself, so that you too will not be tempted. [Galatians 6:1]

One of the primary functions of a pastor is to confront people with the truths in God's Word. Many times it is the most loving thing that can be offered to them. A word of caution however...before you confront someone you need to spend some time on your knees before God to make certain you have a right attitude. I could easily address someone with a wrong attitude, saying something like:

- "How many times have you been told this?"
- "I can't believe you are still making these choices!"
- "What are you thinking?"

That attitude is not loving and the person being confronted will probably not accept the truth that follows. It is important to have a soft heart toward the person you confront. You need to feel God's love toward them. They may still disagree with you or even become angry but they will know that you love them.

You help to disciple someone when you speak the truth in love and offer counsel through times of crisis or trouble. Ultimately the truth found in the Word of God is encouraging and comforting.

The Blessings of Love Among Believers

I believe when a body of believers is committed to loving one another three things will happen in the church:

1. They will find favor with unbelievers.
2. Evangelism will take place in the church.
3. God's power will be released.

Day by day continuing with one mind in the temple, and breaking bread from house to house, they were taking their meals together with gladness and sincerity of heart, praising God and having favor with all the people. And the Lord was adding to their number day by day those who were being saved. [Acts 2:46-47]

First, your love for other believers will affect people outside the church because they will see how you love their family members, friends and neighbors. Curiosity will draw them to church where they will experience the presence of the Holy Spirit. This happens at Foothills all the time. Loving others in Jesus' name attracts people in the world.

Second, your love is a strong evangelistic tool. The scripture you just read in Acts 2 said that the Lord daily increased the number of people being saved. They did not have television, church programs or even a New Testament! They *did* have the gospel of truth and love for one another.

Third, God's power will be released in your midst as you love other believers...and especially as new believers are added to your Christian family.

And the congregation of those who believed were one heart and soul; and not one of them claimed that anything belonging to him was his own, but all things were common property to them. And with great power the Apostles were giving testimony to the resurrection of the Lord Jesus, and abundant grace was upon them all.

[Acts 4:32-33]

When you choose to fear God, obey His Word and love one another, God's Spirit rests in your midst because He is pleased. The presence of His Spirit means His power to perform miracles and save lives will abound in the church.

Loving one another was so important to Jesus that it was the only commandment He gave the disciples shortly before He was crucified. Only blessings can result when you choose to obey His request to love others in the Body of Christ.

The Lord will be blessed, the brethren will be blessed...and you will be blessed, knowing that you are heir to all the promises made to those who choose to fear the Lord.

CHAPTER THIRTEEN

Fearing God Through Forgiveness!

Father, forgive them; for they do not know what they are doing. [Luke 23:34]

Many of the people I counsel in my office are there because of relationship problems. It may be a troubled marriage, conflict between family members, or issues involving people in the church or workplace. The circumstances vary but often there is a common root—*unforgiveness*!

Unforgiveness is a sin that destroys more lives than any disease on earth!

Forgiveness is the best-known fundamental of Christianity— we are fully forgiven by God because of the sacrificial death of Jesus Christ. Yet that is only one facet of forgiveness for the Christian. The believer who desires to obey and fear the Lord must view forgiveness as something *owed* in addition to something received...if you are a Christian you have a responsibility to forgive others just as God has forgiven you.

The Bible says there are terrible consequences that spring from unforgiveness. Galatians 6:7-8 suggests those consequences manifest in the body and mind.

Do not be deceived, God is not mocked; for whatever a man sows, this he will also reap. For the one who sows to his own flesh will from the flesh reap corruption, but the one who sows to the Spirit will from the Spirit reap eternal life.

When a person chooses to act in the flesh and hold unforgiveness toward another they will reap the consequences in their flesh. The cancer of unforgiveness literally eats away at the body, eventually manifesting itself as anger, bitterness, hatred or even physical illness.

The Bible also says that unforgiveness (a sin), hinders God from hearing a believer's prayers:

But your iniquities have made a separation between you and your God, and your sins have hidden His face from you so that He does not hear. [Isaiah 59:2]

Refusing to forgive is *willful* sin and scripture is clear...sin separates you from God and prevents Him from hearing you.

How To Detect Unforgiveness

Jesus Christ promised His followers abundant life [John 10:10] yet countless Christians live in lack and defeat...never understanding why. Often it is because they harbor unforgiveness toward someone and do not even recognize it.

Unforgiveness is easy to detect when it is accompanied by an attitude that seems to say, "I will *never* forgive that person!" Often, however, the unforgiveness that subverts abundant life in Christ is much more subtle. It is *not* a conscious thought or attitude, but has been suppressed or denied. Honest answers to these questions can help reveal areas of unforgiveness:

1. Do you become critical—in thought or words—each time a particular person's name is mentioned?

2. Is there someone you avoid as much as possible?

3. Have you tried your entire life to make certain you are not like your parents?

4. Does anger well up in you when you think about a person who has rejected or hurt you in the past?

5. Do you wrestle with depression?

6. If you were abused as a child, do you frequently think about the abuser?

7. Do you credit someone's actions toward you in the past for the way you are today?

8. Are you angry with someone and feel that you are justified in that anger?

9. Do you think about revenge toward a particular person?

10. Right now as you read these questions do you find yourself thinking, "He just does not understand what was done to me...I have tried to forgive but cannot"?

11. Do any of these questions make you so uncomfortable that you are considering *not* reading the rest of this chapter?

If you answered yes to even *one* of these questions you probably have unforgiveness in your heart. Friend, it is affecting you. Even a tiny bit of unforgiveness permeates a person's entire life...bringing great consequences and grief. I am so convinced of this that every day of my life I pray, "Lord if there is any unforgiveness in my heart I want it out. Reveal it to me so I can forgive!"

Unforgiveness poisons communication with children and a spouse...it breeds anger and bitterness and infects every area of life.

The Hostage of Unforgiveness

During the months following the September 11, 2001 terrorist attack on the United States a journalist named Daniel Pearl was taken hostage in Pakistan. He was an innocent man simply doing his job—reporting on topics related to the tragedy for the Wall Street Journal—when Muslim terrorists kidnapped him. His abduction sparked outrage among people of all races and religions...outrage is a natural response to such a horrendous act.

As is typical when a person is taken hostage, Pearl's abductors made a demand in exchange for his safe release...free all

Pakistanis arrested in connection with the U.S. crackdown on terrorism or Pearl would be killed. The demand was not met and Pearl's captors beheaded him.

The real prisoners were the Muslim terrorists. They remained prisoners of their hatred for Americans and Israelis...Christians and Jews. Had the U.S. released all Pakistani prisoners it would not have been enough. The Muslim extremists would have continued to hate because they are prisoners of unforgiveness.

Whenever a hostage is taken some demand is made as a condition for release of the captive. The demand may be for money, a jet, and passage to some country or the release of criminal cohorts—as in the case involving Daniel Pearl. The specifics of the demands vary, but the basic message is the same..."I will not give back what I have taken until you give me what I want."

A heart that holds unforgiveness is a hostage taker, holding the offender hostage until the demand of their heart is satisfied. An unforgiving heart essentially says, "I will not forgive you until you repay me what I believe you owe me! I will withhold love, acceptance, and forgiveness from you until you repay me." That line of reasoning is flawed because no retribution will ever be enough to satisfy the heart that holds unforgiveness!

Yet there is a second prisoner taken by an unforgiving heart— the one who refuses to forgive. He becomes a prisoner of his own anger, hate, bitterness, and unforgiveness. He will never be free until forgiveness releases him from bondage.

Fearing the Lord Requires Forgiveness

The Bible is very clear...if you want to fear God and live in obedience you have no option other than to forgive. In preparing for this chapter I performed a search on my computer in the New American Standard Bible for the scriptures referencing *forgive, forgives, forgiven, forgiving,* and *forgiveness.* There are more than 100 verses and many of them are directly dealing with a believer's responsibility to forgive!

216

God wants His children to be blessed. When you forgive others He is able to release blessings to you—blessings we will examine later in this chapter. But if you do not forgive there are serious consequences.

The Apostle Paul had a deep understanding of forgiveness for followers of Christ...that it is both *received* through Christ and *owed* to others. In his writings to the Ephesian and Colossian believers he shared his insight into forgiveness and a right relationship with God.

> *Be kind to one another, tender-hearted, forgiving each other, just as God in Christ also has forgiven you.*
> *[Ephesians 4:32]*

> *Bearing with one another, and forgiving each other, whoever has a complaint against anyone; just as the Lord forgave you, so also should you. [Colossians 3:13]*

Paul essentially says, *"Jesus is the example...He forgave us and we must forgive others."* He is applying to forgiveness the principle about love found in 1 John 4:19, which says that we are able to love because God first loved us. We are able to forgive others—and owe them forgiveness—because Jesus first forgave us!

How Much Forgiveness?

When Jesus was with the disciples He addressed the question of how often forgiveness is to be extended:

> *Then Peter came and said to Him, "Lord, how often shall my brother sin against me and I forgive him? Up to seven times?" Jesus said to him, "I do not say to you, up to seven times, but up to seventy times seven." [Matthew 18:21-22]*

When Peter asked the question he probably thought he was being generous in suggesting that forgiveness be offered seven times, but his question held a hidden motive. He was essentially saying, "There is a limit to the number of times I must forgive someone, right?"

217

No doubt Peter was surprised by Jesus' reply. Essentially Jesus said, "You must extend unlimited forgiveness to anyone who asks from his heart to be forgiven!"

By no means did Jesus intend for Peter to keep a record of the number of times he forgave a person until they had been forgiven 490 times...releasing Peter to withhold forgiveness for subsequent offenses.

Jesus made that clear in the parable that followed:

For this reason the Kingdom of Heaven may be compared to a king who wished to settle accounts with his slaves. When he had begun to settle them, one who owed him ten thousand talents was brought to him. But since he did not have the means to repay, his lord commanded him to be sold, along with his wife and children and all that he had, and repayment to be made. So the slave fell to the ground and prostrated himself before him, saying, 'Have patience with me and I will repay you everything.' And the lord of that slave felt compassion and released and forgave him the debt. But that slave went out and found one of his fellow slaves who owed him a hundred denarii; and he seized him and began to choke him, saying, 'Pay back what you owe.' So his fellow slave fell to the ground and began to plead with him, saying, 'Have patience with me and I will repay.' But he was unwilling and went and threw him in prison until he should pay back what was owed. So when his fellow slaves saw what had happened, they were deeply grieved and came and reported to their lord all that had happened. Then summoning him, his lord said to him, 'You wicked slave! I forgave you all that debt because you pleaded with me. Should you not also have had mercy on your fellow slave, in the same way that I had mercy on you?' And his lord, moved with anger, handed him over to the torturers until he should repay all that was owed him. My heavenly Father will also do the same to you, if each of you does not forgive his brother from your heart. [Matthew 18:23-35]

Knowing the value of currency during Jesus' time will help you better understand what the wicked slave received from the king and what he withheld from his fellow slave.

The wages paid to an average worker was one denarius per day...six denarii per week. Six thousand denarii equaled one talent, so it would take the average worker twenty years to earn *one* talent. The wicked slave owed the king ten thousand talents...*two hundred thousand years' wages*!

Peter, a simple fisherman, could not comprehend a debt so great...and that was exactly Jesus' point! He wanted to make it clear that the debt cancelled by the King was beyond human ability to pay.

You and I are better able to appreciate the amount Jesus used by viewing it in terms of its modern equivalent. According to U.S. Census Bureau figures for 2001 the median income for an adult male who works full time is roughly $38,000 per year...$122 per day. The modern equivalent to ten thousand talents is seven billion, six hundred million dollars!

Wages	Ancient Value	Modern Equivalent
1 Day:	1 denarius	$122.00
1 Week:	6 denarii	$732.00
1 Year:	300 denarii	$38,000.00
20 Years:	1 talent	$760,000.00
200,000 Years:	10,000 talents	$7,600,000,000.00

Even a man who earns $150,000 per year today would have to work more than fifty thousand years to earn as much money as the unforgiving servant owed his master.

Jesus' point was about *forgiving* the debt, not repaying it, because it was too great a debt to be repaid by the wicked slave or his descendants for thousands of years.

As you read Jesus' parable you may think, "What a jerk! This slave who has just been released from an immense debt by the king then rushes out to punish a fellow slave for not repaying a small debt!" [The debt of 100 denarii owed by the second slave is equal to about 16 weeks wages.] Yet there is a hard truth in this parable—if you have unforgiveness in your heart toward anyone you are that wicked slave!

Jesus' parable is clear...serious consequences accompany unforgiveness! He said the king turned over the wicked slave to torturers until the full debt could be paid, then Jesus addressed His listeners saying,

And the Lord, moved with anger, handed him over to the torturers until he should repay all that was owed. My heavenly Father will also do the same to you, if each of you does not forgive his brother from your heart.

[Matthew 18:34-35]

Unforgiveness Invites Demonic Influence

God allows torturers to access those who refuse to forgive! The definition of torturer is one who brings pain and toil or distorts or twists the body or mind. These torturers are demonic spirits! A person who harbors unforgiveness in their heart in essence gives the enemy permission to torture their body and mind. If you have ever held unforgiveness toward someone you have probably felt the torturer's attack on your person...you see the one who wronged you and suddenly your mind is flooded with agonizing thoughts—hurtful memories, plots for revenge, or fantasies of justifying yourself. The rancor in your heart causes your stomach to churn and spasm. Your body and mind are under attack by torturers!

The mind surrendered to unforgiveness steeps itself in bitterness and hate...the body driven by bitterness and hate is a breeding ground for all sorts of ills. I believe that some terminal illnesses are brought on by a life of practicing unforgiveness! Unforgiveness is willful sin—and willful sin is an open invitation for Satan to come in and rule the areas not surrendered to God. When a person allows Satan access to their body and mind through unforgiveness it is not unreasonable to think that he would want to bring sickness and death.

In Jesus' parable the king did not desire to hand over the wicked slave to torturers...he wanted to give the man freedom. Yet because the wicked slave chose to punish another for the very thing he had been forgiven...he brought judgment upon himself. He literally delivered himself into bondage! When a person chooses unforgiveness God allows demonic spirits to harass them until they pay in full the debt they owe—forgiveness!

It is amazing the details people remember of offenses suffered ten...twenty...thirty years past. They recall the exact words spoken, the facial expressions and tones of voice used. People who cannot remember where they put their keys five minutes ago will never forget the offense that chains them to unforgiveness. The reason is supernatural—it is a work of hell! Demonic spirits... given access to them when they chose not to forgive...remind them continually of every minute detail. The enemy wants them to replay the incident and relive the pain day after day...year after year until it is chiseled into the stone that was once their heart. Ironically, the person they want to think of least is the one they dwell on most! The result is bitterness and hatred that poison every relationship they have...all they think and do. Their willingness to embrace those memories keeps them in the prison of unforgiveness.

Forgiveness, on the other hand, brings freedom from demonic torment and obsession over the offender. It is amazing how details of an offense—even those replayed in the mind for years—quickly fade and disappear when a person chooses to forgive. God sets a hedge of protection around the forgiver, demonic spirits are barred from access and God cleanses and renews the mind. That, too, is supernatural—it is a work of heaven! Choosing forgiveness is choosing life over death.

I have set before you life and death, blessings and curses.
Now choose life, so that you and your children may live.
[Deuteronomy 30:19 NIV]

Friend, I pray that if you are experiencing consequences of unforgiveness you will yearn so deeply for freedom from demonic spirits that you will be willing to forgive the offender. Forgiveness does not excuse the wrong...it frees you from the wrong. Jesus paid dearly to extend forgiveness—and freedom—to you. Accept and live in that freedom by choosing to forgive others.

Consequences of Unforgiveness

Jesus encouraged His listeners to forgive so that they might avoid the consequences of unforgiveness:

Whenever you stand praying, forgive, if you have anything against anyone, so that your Father who is in heaven will also forgive you your transgressions. But if you do not forgive, neither will your Father who is in heaven forgive your transgressions. [Mark 11:25-26]

This passage can cause confusion if you misinterpret its meaning. It does not mean that Christ reverses the forgiveness of sin you received when you accepted Him as your Savior. Theologians refer to that as positional forgiveness...when you ask Jesus Christ into your heart your *position* before God is one of forgiveness. When God the Father looks at you He sees you through Jesus Christ.

What Jesus means in this passage is that if you do not forgive others, God the Father will not release you from the consequences of your sin of unforgiveness...you will reap the full consequences of what you sow.

Often drug abuse, alcoholism, marital conflicts, low self-esteem, inability to trust or love and endless relationship problems are directly related to unforgiveness!

Unforgiveness can become an infection that craves *excess!* In an attempt to anesthetize the pain inflicted by loved ones many people abuse drugs or alcohol. This may numb the pain for a time but unforgiveness is working in the background to increase the pain...increasing the amount of excess needed to achieve numbness! And often while the hurting person is drunk or high guess what is consuming their thoughts...their pain and the one who caused it!

Excess for some people manifests as overeating or sleeping too much. For others it is complete immersion in sports, entertainment, or exercise. I know a woman who exercises 6 hours every day! There is nothing wrong with these things when used in healthy moderation, but when they are done in excess it is an attempt to suppress pain.

Do you see yourself in the examples listed above? If you do I believe God is using this chapter to speak to you! Perhaps you are in the early stages of unforgiveness and this chapter has caused you to think of someone you need to forgive. Perhaps your wound is recent...someone did or said something hurtful to you. God wants you to get rid of it now! Do not let it linger one moment longer...just forgive! Even if what was done to you was terrible and you are justified in your anger—forgive! Do not choose the path that will poison you for the rest of your life. Make a decision to fear God and forgive...walk away from the consequences because you *can* walk away.

Forgiveness is Freedom

As you sit reading this I want you to say something out loud right now...*forgiveness is freedom*. Speak it out again...*forgiveness is freedom*. If you remember nothing else from this chapter please remember this...*forgiveness is freedom*! Do you want to be free of the past...free from the effects of abuse...free from demonic oppression? *Forgive!*

What Seeds Are You Sowing?

Do not be deceived, God is not mocked; for whatever a man sows, this he will also reap. For the one who sows to his own flesh will from the flesh reap corruption, but the one who sows to the Spirit will from the Spirit reap eternal life. [Galatians 6:7-8]

Unforgiveness is a seed sown in the flesh, so that is where the consequences will be...bitterness, anger and misery.

Forgiveness is a seed sown in the Spirit so a spiritual harvest results...abundant life!

I know a man who has been reaping the bitter fruit of unforgiveness for years. He is over 70 years old and is more angry, bitter, and miserable than any person I have ever known. He does not have a friend in the world. Once I heard him screaming and cursing as he ran down the street in the neighborhood where he lives. He was shouting every foul word imaginable, taking the Lord's name in vain and making obscene gestures with both hands. The veins on his neck popped out as he raged. Everyone in the neighborhood is careful to steer clear of him, though at times many were caught in his cross hairs.

Out of sheer meanness he had his property surveyed and discovered that twenty years earlier his neighbor had erected a fence that was one foot on his side of the property line. He dug up the neighbor's fence and pulled up his irrigation system while his neighbor was at work! Only one thing makes a person that hateful...unforgiveness! It so dominates a person that they often become more bitter, angry, and evil than the person they refuse to forgive! The Bible says,

> *The mouth speaks out of that which fills the heart.*
> *[Matthew 12:34]*

When unforgiveness, bitterness and hate fill a person's heart it eventually flows out of their mouth and contaminates their children, friends, and others around them with bad seeds. The opposite is also true. You can identify a person with a forgiving heart by the things they say...they are people who sow good seeds.

They Do Not Know What They Are Doing!

Jesus was a *perfect* example of this at His death. He had been the target of a conspiracy, falsely accused, lied about, unjustly sentenced to die, and nailed to a cross. Yet His heart was revealed in the words He spoke:

> *They came to the place called 'The Skull' and there they crucified Him and the criminals, one on the right and one*

on the left. But Jesus was saying, "Father forgive them; for
they do not know what they are doing." And they cast lots
dividing up His garments among themselves.
[Luke 23:33-34]

Remember, when Jesus spoke these words His accusers were
standing there mocking Him, blood was trickling from His hands
and feet and He knew that death was near. Yet He did not give in
to anger or unforgiveness...in fact, forgiving at that moment was a
large part of His victory and triumph on the cross!

Jesus' words presented a problem for me until I came to
understand their true meaning. The reason Jesus stated for
asking God to forgive His killers was, *"they do not know what they*
are doing." There have been times when people wronged me,
knowing *exactly* what they were doing...thcy were not sleep-
walking or unconscious! Instead, they made a willful
choice...sometimes a devastating and hurtful choice...to wrong me!

If that has happened to you, you probably felt, as I did, that
anger and unforgiveness toward the offender was justified and the
person needed to *pay* for what they did!

It would be hard enough to say, "Even though you knew what
you were doing I forgive you," but unthinkable to say, "I forgive
you because you *did not know* what you were doing."

Yet that is the absolute truth! The offenders really *did not*
know what they were doing! There is a scriptural principle that
engages when someone wrongs another...it is found in Luke 6:38.
This scripture is usually quoted in teachings about giving but it is
applicable to other actions too.

Give, and it will be given to you. They will pour into your
lap a good measure—pressed down, shaken together, and
running over. For by your standard of measure it will be
measured to you in return. [Luke 6:38]

While this truth is usually applied to our finances it impacts
many other things, including behavior. When a man or woman
spends a lifetime cheating, slandering and abusing others God will

allow that person to receive back what they dished out...in greater measure!

God essentially says, "You get to choose what and how much you receive! Your choice is determined by what you deem acceptable for others...and it will be returned to you *pressed down, shaken together, running over!*"

People who treat others cruelly invite cruelty toward themselves, only in greater measure. One who is abusive, lies, and cheats will be allowed *by God* to suffer at the hands of others who abuse, lie and cheat!

Because of our fallen nature people are basically self-centered. Think about it for a moment...who is always on your mind? [If you answered, "Jesus!" then my response is, "Nice try, but you are not being honest!"] *YOU* are always on your mind just as *I* am always on my mind! That is why we both need Jesus. Without Him it is far too easy for us to be self-absorbed! That is why there are numerous references in the Bible to *dying to self* or *dying to the flesh*...people naturally think of themselves first and most!

Given this level of self-centeredness who would *willingly* mistreat others if they knew that it would come back to them five, ten or twenty times *worse*? Only someone completely ignorant of that truth...someone who *does not know what they are doing!*

Do you see now the deep truth in what Jesus spoke on the cross? People who do terrible things to others have no idea what they are doing...*to themselves!*

If someone has abused you, lied about you, or cheated you, friend, they had no idea what they were doing. They did not know that a judgment fell upon them that they could not escape and in greater measure than they doled out to you.

The biblical truth in Luke 6:38 applies to good things too. If you are kind to others God will pour out *abundant* kindness on you. If you are generous God will return to you generously. God is a God of abundance and He *loves* to lavish on His people good things!

Biblical principles work whether or not you know them... whether or not you are a Christian. The passage in Luke is not the only scripture that links a person's actions to their experience:

However you want people to treat you, so treat them for this is the Law and the Prophets. [Matthew 7:12]

Jesus offers the same basic message...the way you treat others dictates how you will be treated.

When you understand what Jesus' words really meant at the cross it is much easier to apply them when you are wounded...and extend forgiveness to the offender.

Forgiveness Defined

What does it mean to forgive someone? The dictionary defines it this way: *to cease to blame or feel resentment against; to grant pardon; to release a person from debt.* To truly forgive someone you must choose to freely and completely release them from any responsibility *to you* for what they have done.

At the beginning of this chapter you read about the hostage-taking heart that says, "I will not forgive you until you repay me what I believe you owe me!" Here is a sad truth...the unforgiving heart is *never* satisfied so repayment is impossible! No apology is sincere enough...no dollar amount high enough...no pain severe enough...to appease the heart that will not forgive!

Marriage counseling offers a good example...many times I have seen one spouse ask the other to forgive but the wounded spouse refuses! The reason is simple—forgiveness has nothing to do with the offender. It has everything to do with the one being asked to forgive! It is a choice and the One "asking" ultimately is God. Forgiveness is choosing to fear and obey God and live free from anger, bitterness and despair while unforgiveness is choosing to disobey God and live a miserable, bitter life...accumulating one offense after another.

Forgiveness releases the offender from owing any debt to you and places them squarely into the hands of God! Forgiveness essentially says, "I am not your judge...God is your judge! God will deal justly with you as He determines. I do not want this to influence my life now or in the future so I forgive you. You do not understand what you did." The one who responds this way is free! Free from anger and bitterness...free from the consequences of disobeying God's command...free from the daily influence of the offender...free to walk daily in the Spirit of God!

Forgiveness is Simple...Not Easy!

Forgiveness is simple...but that does not mean that it is easy—especially if the tormentors have been hanging around for several years. They do not want to release you! Sometimes a person who has been wounded needs help dealing with unforgiveness. Galatians 6:2 says,

> *Bear one another's burdens, and thereby fulfill the law of Christ.*

Like many churches in the Body of Christ, Foothills Christian Fellowship has a number of ministries that specifically help people learn to choose to forgive. One of the best is a multi-church ministry called Cleansing Stream Ministries, and there are many others; ask your pastor.

If you have unforgiveness *please* ask for help...especially if you are raising children! I guarantee a parent with an unforgiving heart spews out bitterness that pollutes their children! Love your children enough to seek freedom!

Barriers to Forgiveness

There are seven common barriers to forgiveness. Being aware of them can actually help you identify the early stages of unforgiveness and deal with it before the tormentors take you captive.

1. **"Oh, there is nothing to forgive! Don't worry about it."**

That is a subtle deception! You should *choose* to forgive even the smallest infractions, offenses and misunderstandings! Remember—the enemy is running around like a roaring lion trying to find people he can devour, and he frequently gains access to people by pouncing on small issues and making them huge ordeals. He is looking for a weak spot in your life. Do not let him find one! Do not make light of it when someone transgresses you...simply forgive. Choose forgiveness even before they ask for it. If the enemy tries to tempt you with it *remind* yourself that you have already forgiven that person.

2. "Time heals all wounds."

No it does not! It makes the wound worse! The longer those tormentors have access to your life through unforgiveness the more they will pick at the wound until it becomes a festering cancer! Time does not heal all wounds...choosing to forgive heals the wounds.

3. "Forgiveness means I must trust that person again."

Forgiveness and trust are two separate issues. God commands you to forgive others, yet the only One you *must* trust is Him [Proverbs 3:5]! God says you are to be gentle as doves but wise as serpents. You do not have to trust someone who has proven to be untrustworthy...but you must forgive them.

4. "Forgiving is essentially saying, 'What you did was okay'."

Not true! Forgiveness is not an absolution of sin. What the person did may have been completely wrong! They are accountable to God for their wrongdoing and will deal with it in a godly way or suffer consequences! Your forgiveness does not release them from responsibility *for* their actions...it releases you from the effects *of* their actions. By choosing to forgive you are freeing yourself from the damage caused by the wrongdoing and the consequences of unforgiveness!

5. Justifying or excusing someone's behavior.

This differs from barrier number one in that it goes a step beyond brushing off a transgression and justifies it! "Sure, he did a wrong thing but only because *[fill in the excuse]*." This is common

229

and *harmful!* On the surface it may seem benevolent but it provides a weak spot for the enemy to target. If someone offends you...admit it! Do not seek an excuse for the offense...just forgive.

6. Thinking that we must always go to someone to forgive them.

Not true! There are many instances when it would be inappropriate to go to the offender such as when a rape has occurred or in certain abuse cases. There are times when writing a letter or making a phone call may be an option...especially if the offender is a family member, but do it in love. It would be best to seek the wise counsel of leaders or mature Christians before embarking on this attempt.

> *Without consultation, plans are frustrated, But with many counselors they succeed. [Proverbs 15:22]*

There are times when it is impossible to go to the offender, as in cases when the person has died. Forgiveness is a heart issue...just forgive! Even if the offender is dead your heartfelt forgiveness prevents the torturers from having access to you.

7. Pride!

This is the "biggie." When someone has been hurt a prideful attitude perpetuates a state of unforgiveness. "Just who do they think they are doing that to me?" Pride refuses to be humble and freely forgive. The prideful heart says, "They do not *deserve* to be forgiven," but God says He will bless and exalt all who humble themselves before Him and obey His commands!

> *Humble yourselves under the mighty hand of God and He will exalt you. [1 Peter 5:6]*

When you forgive you are humbling yourself before God... submitting to Him...fearing Him! You are choosing to die to self and do as God instructs. Humility before God results in reward:

> *Humble yourselves in the presence of the Lord and He will exalt you. [James 4:10]*

Five Steps of Forgiveness

There are five steps you must take to forgive:

1. Understand that forgiveness is a decision.

It is not a feeling, it is simply dying to self, fearing God and *choosing* to do as He commands. If you are one who says, "I cannot forgive," the truth is you *will not* forgive. God would not command you to do something you are incapable of doing. Since He commands you to forgive, forgiveness is *always* possible! *You **can** do all things through Christ who strengthens you [Philippians 4:13 NKJV]* the question is, "Will you?" His body, the church, can help you work through the process when you choose to forgive.

2. Understand that you are forgiven.

You can forgive because Christ first forgave you. Remember, like the wicked slave you have a debt that has been cancelled. You have transgressed against God much more than anyone will ever transgress against you, yet you have full forgiveness through your Lord and Savior Jesus Christ. You can never repay Him but you can show your appreciation by obeying His command to forgive just as you have been forgiven [Matthew 6:14-15].

3. Release the offender from all debt.

Accept that the offender owes you *nothing* in exchange for forgiveness. Forgiveness is not conditional; it is final and absolute!

4. Accept people as they are.

This is very important! If you wait for someone to change before you forgive you will only hurt yourself. You must forgive them and accept that they are under God's care and control. If change is needed God will oversee that process...and even God gives people the freedom to choose *not* to change. His hope is that they will not make poor choices and suffer consequences but ultimately He allows every person the freedom to choose.

5. View the entire experience as a tool God is using to affect your growth as a Christian.

This is one of the wonderful benefits to being a Christian! Romans 8:28 says:

And we know that God causes all things to work together for good to those who love God, to those who are called according to His purpose.

I love the forgiving heart Joseph displayed toward the brothers who sold him into slavery [Genesis 37-50]. Though he had been mistreated Joseph recognized that God was the One directing his life. He forgave and God was able to bless him, making him ruler over Egypt, second only to Pharaoh. Famine brought Joseph's brothers to Egypt in search of food and he had the power to decide if they should eat or starve...with a word Joseph could have ordered them put to death! Instead he spoke some of the most humble words in all of scripture!

Do not be afraid, for am I in God's place? As for you, you meant evil against me, but God meant it for good in order to bring about this present result, to preserve many people alive. [Genesis 50:19-20]

Forgiveness Makes You More Like Jesus

Friend, you have a promise from God...regardless of what horrible thing has happened to you, if you forgive, God will bless you. Somehow He will miraculously use that experience to improve you and make you more like Jesus than you were before it happened. That may seem unbelievable but it is true! God will transform it into a blessing when you fear Him and obey, forgive the offender and seek to humble yourself under His mighty, merciful hand.

Forgiveness is powerful! It brings healing to you and often brings the offender to repentance and restoration. That is why the enemy works so hard to keep you in bondage to unforgiveness... reminding you how deeply you have been hurt.

God is sovereign. He could have prevented your experience but chose to allow it. [That does not mean He orchestrated it!] All He allows is designed to accomplish the plans He has for your ultimate good!

> *"For I know the plans I have for you," declares the LORD, "plans to prosper you and not to harm you, plans to give you hope and a future." [Jeremiah 29:11 NIV]*

When you choose to fear God and forgive you cooperate with His plans to bless you beyond what you can imagine! Though His plan is custom made for each believer, forgiveness enables God to work His purpose out in our lives.

Remember, forgiveness is freedom!

CHAPTER FOURTEEN

Fear God and Pursue Holiness

Pursue peace with all men, and the sanctification without which no one will see the Lord. [Hebrews 12:14]

If you want to hear God speaking to you, if you want to be close to God, if you want to experience His presence, then pursue holiness.

You also, as living stones, are being built up as a spiritual house for a holy priesthood, to offer up spiritual sacrifices acceptable to God through Jesus Christ.

But you are A CHOSEN RACE, A ROYAL PRIESTHOOD, A HOLY NATION, A PEOPLE FOR God's OWN POSSESSION, that you may proclaim the excellencies of Him who has called you out of darkness into His marvelous light. [1 Peter 2:5,9]

The Bible expects you and I to pursue what God has called us to be. God wants us to say, "Lord, whatever your will is, that's what I want to do in every aspect of my life."

Therefore come out from them and be separate, says the Lord. Touch no unclean thing, and I will receive you.

I will be a Father to you, and you will be my sons and daughters, says the Lord Almighty.
[2 Corinthians 6:17-18]

Paul is quoting from the Old Testament, essentially saying that if we separate ourselves unto God, if we pursue holiness, God will become our Father and we will become like sons and daughters to Him.

Let us cleanse ourselves from all defilement of flesh and spirit, perfecting holiness in the fear of God.
[2 Corinthians 7:1]

If you have made a decision to fear God with your life, pursuing holiness is not an option. Pursuing holiness means that we separate ourselves from practices, activities and relationships which cause us to compromise or rationalize the Word of God.

Why it is Unwise to Compromise

In 2 Kings, chapter 3, we have a very interesting story. The kingdom of Israel has been broken up into a northern and southern kingdom. The northern kingdom at this time is ruled by a King Jehoram who did many good things in the sight of the Lord. He eliminated the worship of Baal, but he failed to eliminate the golden calves in two high places, Dan and Bethel. He kept them so that people would not go to the southern kingdom to worship God at Jerusalem. I'm sure he thought it was a politically expedient to strengthen his reign. He basically said, "You do not have to go to Jerusalem to worship God. We will set up places here because that is a long way for you to travel." These golden calves were first created as just *representations* of God, but eventually people began to worship them as gods, as idols.

Jehoram eliminated Baal, but reintroduced the worship of the two idols in Dan and Bethel. If you visit Israel, go to the city of Dan and you will see the high place where the golden calf rested. In essence, Jehoram compromised the Word of God for political purposes.

In the south was King Jehoshaphat who also had done many things for the Lord, but he "left the high places" where people worshipped idols. These high places were originally built by King Solomon for his many wives who all had these different gods. The high places throughout the kingdom of Judah were for these gods. These high places were probably retained as a matter of political expediency because much of the royalty had their lineage from many of Solomon's wives. It was expedient to leave these high places for the small part of the population who felt they needed their altars.

Both Jehoram and Jehoshaphat left these idols for political reasons, giving the enemy entrance into their kingdoms.

So here is what happened.

The king of Moab rebelled against the king of Israel, King Jehoram. So King Jehoram asks King Jehoshaphat if he will come and help him put down the rebellion. King Jehoshaphat says, "Sure, we'll help you." Next they ask the king of Edom, a small king with a small army, for his help. The forces gather together before the battle, and King Jehoshaphat essentially says, "Listen, we need a prophet of God before we do anything." So they call in Elisha because, 1] they do not have any water, and 2] they want to know what the Lord has to say about the coming battle. Should they attack or not?

Elisha prophesied, essentially saying, "Attack Moab and you will defeat them." He tells them to dig trenches and that God would provide them with water. In obedience they dig the trenches and water comes.

The Moabites think the water is blood because of the way the light was shining on it. They thought that the three kings of the Israelite army had somehow fought amongst themselves, causing the blood to spill over into the water.

But when they [the Moabites] came to the camp of Israel, the Israelites arose and struck the Moabites, so that they fled before them; and they went forward into the land, slaughtering the Moabites. Thus they destroyed the cities; and each one threw a stone on every piece of good land and filled it. So they stopped all the springs of water and felled all the good trees, until in Kir-hareseth [which is the capital of Moab] only they left its stones; [in other words the walls around this city they did not destroy yet]; however, the slingers went about it and struck it [they were throwing large stones against the wall; in other words they were in the process of destroying it]. When the king of Moab saw that the battle was too fierce for him [he decided to save his own skin], he took with him 700 men who drew swords, to break through to the king of Edom [in other words he figured I am going to go through the weakest link here and escape]; but they could not. [Now here's the part that has bothered me ever since the first time that I read it.] Then he took his oldest son who was to reign in his place, and offered him as a burnt offering on the wall. And there came great wrath against Israel, and they departed from him and returned to their own land. [2 Kings 3:24-27]

There is a great warning for us in this passage. Notice that after the king sacrificed his son, "a great wrath came against Israel" and they retreated. Israel had totally defeated the Moabites until the King of Moab sacrificed his son. Then, a great demonic wrath came against Israel and they were not able to stand against it.

Why weren't God's people able to withstand that attack of the enemy?

Because they had polluted and compromised God's Word. The lesson here is clear: when you and I have a practice, a relationship or an activity in our lives that compromises or rationalizes God's Word, it is a sin, and that sin opens a gap in our spirit for Satan to march in and out of at will.

Sin and compromise give the devil an entrance into our life.

Close the Sin Gap!

If you are practicing sin right now, you have given the enemy access to your life, just as the two kings did. When there is an attack from the enemy, you have lost your spiritual armor and the spiritual fortitude to push back the attack. That's why the troops ran away.

So often I see Christians who are involved in an activity, relationship or in some rationalization or compromise that opens to door to allowing Satan to hit them, and they fall. Stop the sexual immorality, the lying—any sin will remove your protective spiritual armor and give the devil an opening.

God responds to those who are pursuing Him, not embracing compromise and disobedience [Revelation 3:16]. If you want God's power manifested in your life, the power to resist temptation, the power to overcome bondages, then separate yourself from sin.

If the Church wants to see God's Spirit moving powerfully, then the Body of Christ and the leaders of the Church must be separated from practices, relationships and activities that cause us to compromise God's Word.

Listen to that Still, Small Voice

For the grace of God has appeared, bringing salvation to all men, instructing us to deny ungodliness and worldly desires and to live sensibly, righteously and godly in the present age. [Titus 2:11-12]

When I became a Christian, this was one of the first verses I memorized. When you give your life to Jesus Christ, God's Spirit comes into your life to instruct you to deny ungodliness and worldly desires. God puts a desire in your heart to pursue holiness because He knows it is best for you.

As you pursue holiness, you learn to listen to that still, small voice of God living inside of you, telling you, "Do not go there. Don't do that! Go to a pastor about this situation." Many Christians wear T-shirts and bracelets with the initials W.W.J.D. on them. These initials stand for "What would Jesus do?" Pursuing holiness is asking that question in every aspect of your life.

God is the rewarder of those who seek Him [Hebrews 11:6].

One who pursues holiness says, "Lord, is this what You want me to do?"

James 2 tells us: *"Faith without works is dead."*

Your faith must have the pursuit of holiness to be a "live" faith. If there is an activity, practice or a relationship in your life that you know God is not pleased with, there is a deadness to your

239

faith. You are going to have a hard time hearing God. When you pray and ask God for something, His Holy Spirit is going to respond, "You know, I love you, but get this sin fixed."

Sin causes separation between you and God [Isaiah 59:2].

I believe that the fear of God is missing in the American Church, and without that fear of God, we are more vulnerable to sin, which separates us from God and opens the door to the enemy.

Without the fear of God, revival will never happen.

Too many in the American Church believe they can disobey and rationalize God's Word and not suffer the consequences. They mistakenly think, "Everything's fine. God understands, and He gives me grace."

The one who believes in the Son of God has the witness in himself; the one who does not believe God has made Him a liar, because he has not believed in the witness that God has borne concerning His Son. [1 John 5:10]

The Holy Spirit gives witness in your spirit when you should be doing something or not be doing something, when you should be participating in something or not participating in something. At your job, if something is questionable and you know in your spirit that you should not be participating in it, then stop it or get out! If some "friend" keeps luring you to do things you know you should not be doing, drop the friend.

The Truth and Evidence of God

And I will ask the Father, and He will give you another Helper, that He may be with you forever; that is the Spirit of truth, whom the world cannot receive, because it does not behold Him or know Him, but you know Him because He abides with you, and will be in you. [John 14:16-17]

The Holy Spirit is our helper, the Spirit of Truth. He helps you and I know where we should go and what we should do. He helps us walk in the one truth: God's Word.

*For all who are being led by the Spirit of God, these are
sons of God. [Romans 8:14]*

The pursuit of holiness is evidence that the Holy Spirit lives
inside of you and that you have been born again. When I was
saved at 22 years old, I knew something was radically different
because my filthy mouth changed. I used the name of the Lord
God in vain all the time, and it did not bother me at all. After I
was saved, the very next day every time I even heard someone
take God's name in vain, it hurt me. Now I did not want to curse
anymore. Suddenly I knew it was wrong.

Do not let someone else put what they think is right or wrong
on you; God will tell you. His Word is not rules and regulations,
but about how to pursue Him and know Him with your whole
heart. That's holiness.

Jesus calls us to be the salt of the earth [Matthew 5]. The
Apostle Paul describes us as bright lights to a darkened, perverse
generation [Philippians 2:15]. Clearly, God expects us to be
separate and holy. To be different, we must learn to hear the
"witness" in our spirit, to listen to the Lord when He says, "Do not
read that. Do not go there. Get out of that relationship. Stay in
that marriage."

Expect Persecution for Christ

If you pursue holiness, you will stand out and be persecuted!

In the State of California, statistics tell us that less than 10%
of the population goes to a Christian church. So, when you pursue
holiness, you will be separate.

Pursuing God and separating ourselves from the world is not
easy.

*And indeed, all who desire to live godly in Christ Jesus will
be persecuted. [2 Timothy 3:12]*

If you make a decision to follow Christ with your whole life, you
will be persecuted. Even in the so-called "Christian seminary"

I attended, I experienced persecution and ridicule for my foundational beliefs. So, persecution will come, even in the church. As a pastor, I know there are people who literally hate me because I have said, "This is what the Word of God says about your life." Some write me hate letters, others have spoken badly about me to others and for one reason: I was willing to share Matthew 18 to them, confronting their sin...they just didn't like it. One particular person who I know dislikes me and never speaks well of me...they have *anger* against me. This particular person sat in my office a few years ago weeping and crying and praying for her husband's salvation. He finally surrendered to Jesus but she had already made a decision. Now she wanted to divorce him, she was sick and tired of him period, so, it was over. When I tried to come to her with the Word of God or remind her of her prayers for her husband's salvation, she went ballistic on me. Know that when you make a decision to follow Christ with all your heart some people might not like it, but many will see something different. Listen, if you pursue holiness with your whole life I guarantee you will affect those around you and I guarantee you something else...if you really pursue God with your whole life, people will get saved, they will become Christians because of your life. You will have the awesome joy of bringing neighbors, co-workers or family members to church and seeing them come to the Lord Jesus Christ simply because you have made a decision to pursue holiness.

Nation-changing Christians

If you look through history, what group of people in western civilization has been at the forefront of most of the positive sociological changes in the last thousand years?

Christians!

We have been pioneers in stopping slavery, in improving medicine, in establishing democracy, in creating child labor laws and fighting for women's rights [they being equal under the law], etc.

The real hope for America does not lie in our politicians, it rests with the Church and God's people. This country was never meant to run without a god-fearing population. For example, if you do not believe there is a God, then the whole justice system falls, since it is based upon "Will you tell the truth, the whole truth, so help you God?"

Our democracy, our Constitution, our founding fathers presupposed a god-fearing population. Now, if only 10% of the Californians are going to church on Sunday morning, that gives me pause to be concerned. Our business structure will not work, our government will not work, without a belief in God.

There is little integrity in business anymore. When I was building our home, many of the construction workers consistently lied to me every day in every way.

Christians are challenged to be the salt of the earth. To be that salt, we must stay away from sin and pursue holiness. If you want to know Jesus like you have never known Him before, to know His joy and peace...if you want a strong and blessed marriage, pursue holiness, pursue God.

Release Holy-Spirit Change Now!

I WILL DWELL IN THEM AND WALK AMONG THEM; AND I WILL BE THEIR GOD, AND THEY SHALL BE MY PEOPLE. Therefore, COME OUT FROM THEIR MIDST AND BE SEPARATE," says the Lord. "AND DO NOT TOUCH WHAT IS UNCLEAN; And I will welcome you. And I will be a father to you, And you shall be sons and daughters to Me, says the Lord Almighty.
[2 Corinthians 6:16-18]

THEREFORE, since we have so great a cloud of witnesses surrounding us, let us also lay aside every encumbrance, and the sin which so easily entangles us, and let us run with endurance the race that is set before us.
[Hebrews 12:1]

If you have a practice, an activity or a relationship you need to stop, do it now. Your compromise [sin] opens you up for deception in other areas of your life. Most often when we counsel people here at the church who are experiencing serious problems, it's usually a result of compromise or disobedience to God's Word.

243

Why suffer any more consequences? Pursue your holiness and experience the abundant life God has for you.

Right now come before Jesus and humbly confess your compromise and disobedience before Him remembering that:

> *If we confess our sins, He is faithful and righteous to forgive us our sins and to cleanse us from all unrighteousness. [1 John 1:9]*

And begin right now to pursue holiness, pursue living for God. You'll never be sorry!

CHAPTER FIFTEEN

Worship and Fearing the Lord

How will the fear of God impact your worship?

Remember, fearing God is understanding that what you sow you reap. When you obey God you are blessed, and when you disobey God there are always consequences.

The word "worship" in the Old Testament is "sayha" which means "to bow down, to prostrate before." In the New Testament, the word "proscanio" means the same thing, "bowing down" before someone who has supreme authority over your life. In Bible times, people would bow down before statues, kings, or whoever had ultimate authority in their lives.

Each of us worships the person or thing that holds the highest priority in our life.

We all will worship something because we were made to worship, be it our job, a possession, a pleasure, or a prestige. All the decisions you make in your life are based on that priority.

Some people worship themselves. Everything is "I, I, I" or "Me, me, me." Their primary questions are, "How will I benefit from this?" or "What can you do for me?"

What or Who is Important to You?

In Psalm 115, King David writes about idols made out of wood and stone, silver and gold—things made by men's hands.

They have mouths, but they cannot speak; They have eyes, but they cannot see; They have ears, but they cannot hear; They have noses, but they cannot smell; They have hands, but they cannot feel; They have feet, but they cannot walk;

They cannot make a sound with their throat. Those who make them will be like them, and so will all who trust in them. [Psalm 115:4-8]

David is essentially saying, "It is stupid to worship something [an idol] made by human hands. You will assume the character of the object idol, without the ability to speak or see or hear. You will become cold and hard."

When we worship a person, place or thing, it dictates who we become. All our decisions are based on what we worship, what we value most, be it a job, money, possessions or a person.

I pray that all reading this book will make a decision to worship God as the first priority in your life.

Becoming Your Idol

Look what happens when you worship the wrong god.

For example, if you worship money, that is all you will think about. Eventually, you will become cold, unemotional and hard. All the decisions in your life will be based upon "How much money will this make me?" You will have a terrible time with relationships because money will be more important to you than a wife or family. In America, the money god is one of our largest idols, and dominates many families.

If you worship pleasure, you will be controlled by your emotions, your urges, by what feels good. You will not be controlled by logic, common sense, or by what the Bible says. You will ask, "What makes me feel good?" "What pleases my heart?" Pleasure is a very dangerous god because the Bible says,

The heart is more deceitful than all else it is desperately sick, who can understand it? [Jeremiah 17:9]

Or, you may worship yourself. If all you ever think about is yourself, and every decision you make is about you, pretty soon you become a picture of selfishness and nobody wants to be around you.

If you worship prestige, you will always worry about what other people think about you. "How is this going to advance where I am in the world?" What a lifelong bondage!

But, if you make God the first priority in your life, He will transform you into His image! God's Spirit will change you. One of the most amazing things I have seen as a pastor is that when people really get serious about God, worshipping Him with all their heart, He radically changes them.

As a pastor, one of my frustrations, especially in marriage counseling, is when one spouse yields to the Lord, allowing Him to change their behavior, but the other spouse is so filled with anger and bitterness that they cannot see or accept that change, thus missing the miracle God wants to do in their marriage.

"Must" Worship

In John 4, we see Jesus outside a city called Sychar. While at the well, Jesus holds a conversation with a Samaritan woman. During the course of this conversation they start to talk about worship. Jesus tells her,

> *Yet a time is coming, and has now come, when the true worshippers will worship the Father in spirit and truth, for they are the kind of worshippers the Father seeks. God is spirit, and his worshippers must worship in spirit and in truth. [John 4:23-24]*

God is Spirit, and those who worship Him must worship Him in spirit and in truth. Please circle, underline, highlight, or star the word "must" in your Bible. Jesus is essentially saying, "If you want to worship God, you MUST worship Him one way: in spirit and truth."

The word "must" is only used three times in the Gospel of John:

1.   John 3:7: You MUST be born again.

There is no other way to God, no other way to have communion with Him, no other way to experience forgiveness, no other way to have access to the Father, no other way to have God's Spirit living inside of you, than through Jesus Christ. You *must* acknowledge Him as Lord and Savior. When you do, His Spirit comes inside you.

2.   <u>John 12:34: The Son of Man MUST be lifted up</u>.

There is no other way for salvation to come to mankind, no other way for forgiveness to come to mankind except that Jesus takes the sin of man upon Himself and dies on a cross.

3.   <u>John 4:24: You MUST worship God in Spirit and truth</u>.

Since therefore, brethren, we have confidence to enter the holy place by the blood of Jesus, by a new and living way which He inaugurated for us through the veil, that is, His flesh, and since we have a great priest over the house of God, let us draw near with a <u>sincere</u> heart in full assurance of faith, having our hearts sprinkled clean from an evil conscience and our bodies washed with pure water. [Hebrews 10:19-22]

The word "sincere" is a very important word because, if you have a King James Bible, that word is translated "true." In the New King James Bible and in the Living Bible it is "truth." In the Amplified Bible it is "sincere and honest." So, the word can be translated "sincere, true, truth, honest."

Whatever word you select, the resounding truth here is that if you want to draw near to God, you *must* have a true, sincere, and honest heart.

"Heart" Worship

When the Bible talks about the heart, it means the mind, the emotions and the will. The mind is how we think; the emotions are how we feel; the will is how we make decisions. To manifest a true, honest heart before God, we must submit and surrender to God our thinking, our feelings and our need to make our own decisions.

These people honor me with their lips, but their hearts are far from me. They worship me in vain: their teachings are but rules taught by men. [Matthew 15:8-9]

To worship God with a true and honest heart, you must completely surrender your intellect, emotions and will. Your thoughts must be dictated by what the Word of God says.

You may not like a person at work, but the only question that matters is, "How does God tell me to feel about him in His Word? Every decision you make should be dictated by the Word of God.

In Matthew 15, Jesus quotes from Isaiah 29:13-14:

These people come near to me with their mouth and honor me with their lips, but their hearts are far from me. Their worship of me is made up only of rules taught by men.

If you do not surrender to God you cannot enter into worship. I do not care how much you say you love God, or how many services you go to, or how much you sing praises to Him, you will never enter into worship without surrender, without a true heart.

Worship first and foremost is an attitude of the heart.

Dead Unto Life

Many Christians do not experience God because their hearts are divided...there is something else that takes first place in their life.

God will not tolerate any rivals!

If you want to be a worshipper of God, you must worship Him in how you think, how you feel, how you make decisions.

Paul challenges us to be a living sacrifice. One thing about a sacrifice...it is dead. You must die to the way you want to feel, and how you want to make decisions, and come alive to what God wants you to do.

Now, please do not come under condemnation. We all sin. But you still must want, with every inch of your being, to surrender how you think, feel and make decisions.

Then, when the Holy Spirit does convict us of sin in our lives we should acknowledge it, ask for forgiveness and then seperate ourselves from it.

There is only one person who can separate and keep you from experiencing God, from entering into worship...and that is you! God is always ready to open His door.

Worship in Spirit

God is Spirit.

Since He is Spirit, you and I communicate with God through the Spirit. That is why He has placed His Spirit within us.

On that day you will realize that I am in my Father, and you are in me, and I am in you. Whoever has my commands and obeys them, he is the one who loves me. He who loves me will be loved by my Father, and I too will love him and show myself to him. [John 14:20-23]

Do you see it? God makes His abode with us, literally coming inside of us.

But he who unites himself with the Lord is one with him in spirit. [1 Corinthians 6:17]

When you join yourself with the Lord, you become one spirit with Him. There is a connection. When the Holy Spirit comes into your life, the Spirit literally becomes a roadway, a doorway into the throne room of God.

In him and through faith in him we may approach God with freedom and confidence. [Ephesians 3:12]

If you are born again, you can have access to God whenever you want. Worship is in the spirit, and opens the door to God's throne room.

When you place [submit] anything before God—your job, your homework, your daily exercise, your marriage—it becomes worship.

If you go to God in truth, giving up how you think, feel, and make decisions...totally submitted to Him through the Spirit, you can enter into His throne room. When you do what the Bible tells you, even when you do not feel like doing it, your action becomes worship. In essence, your entire life can be an act of worship. Worshipping God can actually become a lifestyle.

The Multiplied Worship of the Church

If a large percentage of every church in America would come together on Sunday morning with our hearts surrendered to God, our thoughts, our feelings, and how we make decisions fully surrendered to God, when the music starts and we begin praising Him, the church body will be ushered into the throne room of God. In His throne room, you are literally standing right before God, telling Him how wonderful He is. When that happens, He responds by releasing His presence upon those who are worshipping.

God is enthroned on the praises of his people.
[Psalm 22:3]

Through our worship, God literally comes to visit and minister. He responds to worship.

What happens when your church unites together to enter into worship?

God's presence is multiplied! The level of the Holy Spirit begins to rise in the sanctuary. The service becomes a divine appointment with God. That's why it is so important not to miss church, even when you do not feel like coming. In the process of worshipping, God meets us.

There may be some times when you do not feel like coming to church. But, if worship is your habit, and the habit of your church, if you are surrendered in your mind and feelings, you will come, no matter how you feel.

If you are feeling low, and come to church anyway, God can minister to your spirit through those around you who are worshipping the Lord, raising up their hands and singing. They will literally drag you right into the throne room with them because the spirit of God is present.

This is how revival happens!

People will be saved, healed, delivered and convicted in worship. It is not great preaching, good music, new carpet, or great marketing that brings revival. If those things could bring revival, America would be rocking for Jesus! In the last 2000 years there has never been a generation of Christians who have been exposed to as many techniques and programs and teaching materials as we have.

America has beautiful buildings, great marketing techniques, and advertising, but are we winning America?

Not really.

We cannot do it through our own strength or clever techniques.

Revival Worship

I have ministered in Cuba, where the churches have some of the worst musicians I have ever heard. Although the music is frequently terrible, the presence of God is overwhelming because the people worship unlike anything I've ever experienced. They enter into worship and God's presence rocks the place.

America will not see revival until a significant number of Christians in local churches get serious about worship [which brings the presence of God]. If we experience God's presence, if we have Him present in great power, then we become a powerful witness to the non-believers.

You can bring your neighbors to a church that worships.

Even if they have a bad impression of the building or the preaching, they will sense the presence of God...nothing can compare with the presence of God.

Worship is not a philosophy or religion, but an experience of God's presence. Worship brings the Kingdom of God; the Kingdom of God is simply the presence of the King. Where God is present, so too is His Kingdom.

I have been praying for over 20 years that we would see revival here in the East County of San Diego. I look forward to a time when our church is baptizing multitudes of people every week, but that will never happen unless we become sold-out worshippers of God.

When you study the history of revival, you learn that what changed people and cities was the presence of God. His presence would rest on an entire community. People were so on fire for Him that the Spirit of God was everywhere.

The early Church eventually took over the whole known world and made a tremendous impact. The Bible shares how they turned the world upside down!

The Only Way to Revival

While a Jesus video is good, and crusades are important, deep, long-lasting revival is always launched by one thing...the power and presence of God.

The Apostle Paul was not a very good speaker...he admits it!

My message and my preaching were not with wise and persuasive words, but with a demonstration of the Spirit's power, so that your faith might not rest on men's wisdom, but on God's power. [1 Corinthians 2:4-5]

When Paul told the people about Jesus, God's presence was there convicting men's hearts, healing people.

The Kingdom of God went with Paul wherever he went.

For the kingdom of God is not a matter of talk but of power. [1Corinthians 4:20]

God's presence causes things to happen.

Wherever Jesus Christ went, important things happened. When Jesus showed up, things happened. He was not an easy yawn where you spend an hour and a half with Him and then go out to lunch.

For our gospel did not come to you in word only but in the power and the holy spirit and with full conviction.
[I Thessalonians 1:5]

Revival won't come through great preaching. America has experienced some of the greatest preachers who ever lived, but revival's not here yet. Think of all the crusades Billy Graham has conducted with millions of people attending. Yet, Modern America has not experienced revival.

The early Church won their world, won their lost, delivered the demonized, healed the sick through the power and presence of God working through their lives. They brought the presence of God wherever they went because they worshipped in spirit and in truth.

Embers or Flames?

Let me share a story that illustrates the importance of corporate worship.

One winter the pastor went to visit a member who had been missing church more Sundays than not. This gentlemen had a big fire blazing in the fireplace. When he and the pastor began to talk, the man began to share with the pastor. "I really don't need to go to church to worship God. God knows my heart." He told the pastor that he had a little worship and prayer service in his home, all by himself.

In a moment of inspiration, the pastor took a fireplace tong out and put it into the roaring fire. There were some glowing embers at the bottom of the fireplace, so he took out one red-hot ember and put it on the hearth. Then, he put the tong back without saying a word. The two men then watched the hot ember get colder and colder until it was completely out. The man looked at his pastor and said, "I'll be at church Sunday."

When we worship together it brings God's presence, healing, deliverance, inspiration, motivation. Worship is one of the most important reasons we come together, because it brings a powerful presence of the Holy Spirit.

Worship brings the Kingdom of God.

Worship brings revival.

The greatest blessing we have in the Body of Christ is God's presence. It has enabled people to endure hardships for Jesus, to do things far beyond what they could ever normally do. Worship helps you overcome anything. It will give you victory over anything.

You can do all things through Christ's spirit who strengthens you.

STUDY GUIDE

WEEK ONE

READ CHAPTERS 1-3

CHAPTER 1

The Fear of the Lord Produces Knowledge and Wisdom

1. What is the significance of convictions and preferences in a Christian's life?

2. Have you ever compromised God's Word to obtain what you wanted? Write them down and ask God to forgive you.

3. What is the difference between knowledge and wisdom in relation to God's Word?

4. The Bible frequently uses the word "fear". How should that Word be interpreted or defined?

5. What are the two basic truths that define the fear of the Lord?

6. When you consider fearing the Lord in terms of understanding that there are consequences for disobedience and blessings for obedience, can you see examples of this in your own life, others, or in the church?

CHAPTER 2

Fear of the Lord Blessing or Consequence?

1. Why is fearing the Lord so important if a Christian wants to experience the "abundant life" Jesus promises us in John 10:10?

2. Why do you think some Christians think that they will never suffer consequences for their disobedience to God's Word?

3. How would you define "cheap grace"?

4. How does a person hate knowledge and choose not to fear God?

5. Why can't you trust your own heart when making decisions concerning your life?

CHAPTER 3

Fear That Produces Appreciation of God

1. In your own words, how would you describe God? If a non-believer asked you to describe God, what would you say?

2. Define the following words when applied to God: Eternal, Trinity, Omniscient, Omnipresent, and Omnipotent.

3. According to Ephesians 3:20, how does God answer our prayers?

4. Why do you appreciate your Lord Jesus?

5. Now that you have read the first three chapters, what has the Lord shown you about your commitment to Him?

WEEK TWO
READ CHAPTER 4-5

CHAPTER 4

Learning to Fear the Lord

1. Why do you think God ordained that there be twice as many scriptures about fearing Him than about His love?

2. In your own words, why must the fear of the Lord be learned?

3. What are the four ways we learn to fear God and which of them are the hardest for you to commit to? Why?

4. Faith is required to obey God, but what part of God's character do we have faith in?

5. Has peer pressure ever dictated how you made a decision? If so, how? How would you have done it differently if you had feared God?

6. Make a list of idols that American Christians struggle with. After making the list, spend a few minutes praying about your temptations in any of those areas.

7. Why do you believe that American Christians struggle with developing a regular time of Bible study?

Chapter 5

Fearing God with Your Finances

1. Fearing God with our finances begins with biblical stewardship. What does this mean?

2. What part of your income has the Lord God called holy to Himself (Leviticus 27:30)?

3. In Malachi 3:7-12, God makes four statements about the tithe. What are they?

4. How have any one of God's four statements about the tithe affected you, someone you know, or the church you attend?

5. Why is tithing really a test of our hearts?

6. Why is the command to tithe in the Old Testament as relevant today as it was in the Old Testament?

7. Why are we New Testament Christians held to a higher standard than God's people who lived during Old Testament times? How does this apply to our finances?

8. How has God proved His faithfulness in your finances?

WEEK THREE
READ CHAPTER 6-7

CHAPTER 6

Fearing God by Reading His Word

1. What is the formula for failure?

2. Why do so many people believe that large sections of the Bible are not for today?

3. Why would you say that the Bible is the most practical book ever written?

4. Has developing a daily Bible reading schedule been hard for you? Why?

5. Why is it important to understand your life from God's perspective?

6. Why is it extremely important for Christians to know what they believe?

7. What are some of the ways you've seen people pervert or compromise the Word of God?

8. What is the recipe for success?

9. Why is it important to know what the Bible says if you want to be able to witness to others about our Lord Jesus?

CHAPTER 7

The Importance of Prayer for Those Who Fear the Lord

1. In James 4:2, what does the Apostle James say is the secret to God's power and influence being released in your life?

2. Why is daily prayer vital for any Christian who wants to live God's abundant life?

3. Give some examples of how God has answered your prayers.

4. Why is prayer the battleground for what happens in our world?

5. For you, what is the hardest aspect of persevering in prayer?

6. What are the two essential elements to developing a daily discipline of prayer?

7. Have you implemented these two elements into your prayer life? If so, how? If not, how do you propose to do so?

WEEK FOUR
READ CHAPTER 8-9

CHAPTER 8

Fearing the Lord Involves Respecting God's Delegated Authority

1. What is one of Satan's greatest weapons to neutralize the Church in order to keep them from ministering to the world around them? Have you ever seen this happen? How?

2. What is the major responsibility of leaders in the Church? How can we make their jobs easier?

3. Are you willing to submit to God's delegated authority in your life? If so, make a list of God's delegated authority in your life.

4. If you come across someone who is sowing discord and dissension in the Church what should you do?

5. Have you learned anything new about how to respond to God's delegated authority? If so, what?

6. Take a few moments and pray for your Pastor, Assistant Pastors and other church leadership.

CHAPTER 9

Fearing God in Marriage

1. Why is there hope for any troubled marriage?

2. What are most people's attitudes concerning divorce? As a Christian what should our attitude be?

3. In Ephesians 5:22-33, Paul gives us the three foundational truths concerning marriage. List each one and then mention the one aspect of each truth that caught your attention.

4. What would keep a married couple from practicing the 555 Marriage Plan discussed in Chapter 9?

5. Will you make a commitment with your spouse to begin the 555 Marriage Plan in your own marriage? Give a testimony to the group of what has happened as you have begun to spend this time with your spouse.

WEEK FIVE
READ CHAPTER 10-11

CHAPTER 10

The Responsibilities of a Father

1. When a father abdicates his responsibility to his children how does this manifest itself in the child's life? Can you think of any examples?

2. Proverbs 13:22 tells us that a good man leaves an inheritance to his children's children. Practically, how would you see this manifest itself in a family?

3. Ephesians 6:4 tells fathers not to provoke their children to anger and Colossians 3:21 tells fathers not to exasperate their children. In your opinion, what does this mean? What would be the results of obeying or disobeying this Biblical command?

4. List the six responsibilities of a father and briefly describe each.

CHAPTER 11

The Four Responsibilities of a Mother

1. In your own words, what does it mean for a wife to respect her husband? Why would this be hard for some wives?

2. After reading this chapter, how is a wife to love her husband?

3. How does a mother practically manifest her love for her children?

4. Why is it important for a mother to exemplify contentment in the home?

5. What does it mean to form a child's spiritual appetite? Why is this important?

6. If someone asked you to define self-control, what would you say? Why is this characteristic so important for children to learn?

WEEK SIX
READ CHAPTER 12-13

CHAPTER 12

Fearing God by Loving Others

1. In John 13:34-35 Jesus gave us a new covenant. Put this commandment in your own words and explain what it means to you.

2. Why do we need a power greater than ourselves to consistently love one another? Give an example of a time when you knew God was calling you to love. What did you do?

3. Why must our focus always be on Jesus when we love the brethren?

4. What are the two basic ways that we love one another? Give a few examples of each.

5. In your own words, what happens when Christians take seriously Jesus' command to love one another?

CHAPTER 13

Fearing God Through Forgiveness

1. When you choose not to forgive someone, how do you literally hold that person hostage?

2. Serious consequences accompany unforgiveness; Jesus says that the one who refuses to forgive is handed over to torturers. Explain what this means.

3. As He was being crucified at the cross Jesus stated, "Father, forgive them for they do not know what they are doing." What did Jesus mean by this statement? How does this truth affect people who sin against you?

4. There are some common barriers to forgiveness. Can you think of any concrete examples of any of the seven barriers to forgiveness?

5. After reading this chapter, how has the Holy Spirit identified unforgiveness in your heart? What are you going to do about it?

6. Remembering forgiveness is freedom...what does this statement mean to you?

WEEK SEVEN
READ CHAPTER 14-15

CHAPTER 14

Fear God and Pursue Holiness

1. Pursuing holiness means that we separate ourselves from practices, activities and relationships that cause us to compromise or rationalize the Word of God. Give examples of this.

2. As a Christian, what are the major dangers or consequences for hanging on to or practicing sin?

3. Can you think of an example when God's Spirit convicted you concerning an activity, conversation or relationship?

4. If you pursue holiness and truly desire to live for God, what one thing can you count on in varying degrees (2 Timothy 3:12)?

5. Have you ever been persecuted for taking a stand for Christ? If so, when?

CHAPTER 15

Worship and Fearing the Lord

1. We cannot worship God (make Him first priority) if there is an idol in our life. There is an easy way to find out if one exists in your life. Ask yourself, "What in my life keeps me from doing what God wants?" If you can identify something, you've found an idol.

2. Worship, first and foremost, is an attitude of the heart. What does this mean?

3. How can one's everyday life be an act of worship?

4. Why is God's presence multiplied when we come together for worship?

5. Explain this truth: Worship brings the Kingdom of God.

6. Why is God's presence so important when we meet together in small or large groups?

To order additional copies of:

The Fear of the Lord
&
Prayer Will Change Your World

Order From Publisher:

Have your credit card ready and call: Toll free: [866] 484-6184
You may also log onto their website at: www.csnbooks.com

Order From Author:

Phone: [619] 442-7728, ask for special quantity discount pricing.

US Mail:

Fill out form below and send with check made payable to:

David Hoffman
c/o Foothills Christian Fellowship
350 Cypress Lane, Suite B
El Cajon, CA 92020

For *Prayer Will Change Your World* please enclose $9.95. For
The Fear of the Lord please enclose $18.95. Enclose $2.50 for
shipping (if ordering over 3 books, please add $1.00 per each book
for shipping).

Qty.	Description	Price	Total
		Shipping	
		Total